Flight of Freedom

Finding Freedom and Happiness Within

by
U. E. David MBA, MDiv.

Flight of Freedom

Finding Freedom and Happiness Within

Acknowledgments

The stillness that emerges when a journey is finally complete can be an opportunity to reflect and thank. Just as a butterfly comes to rest in some bloom after its difficult journey for transformation, now I reach this page and rest here with all my gratitude. Many people are behind these words, and each person is essential to make the whole. Without them, life would not be as colorful.

First, thank you to those who could not whisper from their "self" during early dawn or late watches and danced around your shadow. O old trees that surround my window thank you for being strong and creating such a lasting impression by having deep roots. "Even of the strongest, we all bend in the storm but still again when winds have ceased to blow us." You added am all warm thinking of my family. I'm indebted to my teenage daughter. This is due to her zeal and interest, which inspired me to embark on this course. Favor Udoh, thank you for instigating me into butterfly research and recording the wisdom found in their nature within the pages of this book.

I also want to appreciate my wife, Prophetess Ayi Udoh, for her sage counsel and solid backing as we embark on this great enterprise of giving the world something they have never seen. However, your support throughout the years gave me the confidence to publish. Your motivations and unwavering love made me write this testimony. I Love You More. Your trust in me and constant encouragement enabled me to finish this book.

My well-wishers, your gentle attitude and divergent consideration, smiles, and/ or words have filled my soul. You demonstrated how our common ideas could fertilize each other, pollinate, and make this book spring.

To Gospel House Revival Ministries (GHRM), the silent masters of my actions, thank you. You've motivated me to look at life with more sense and dream bigger. You are the best; our journey has given me more than what I learned in college.

My editor, your shaper of words and ink surgeon who slices through to inject meaning where none had been before, has improved this piece of art beyond my worst fears. We were in this dance of celebration for the artistry present, and by it, I'm better.

To the multitude of those whose tales and lives have merged this work, who sought change knowing one would go through pain –you are pupa wisdom. Every book's uniqueness arises from you revealing your fragility and boldness with life as it happens. It was proofreaders, enthusiastic typographers, and printers who helped to turn these ideas into a book that you can touch, feel, and have its weight in hand and keep. Your work is the cocoon that brings forth your word.

My critiques and challenges inspire gratitude. Every challenge, like the caterpillar's battle out of its cocoon, has built me muscles and taught me the tenacity I didn't know I had. I am thankful for the many challenges that have led to our brighter wings. It may be the struggle and beauty of the everyday things that we find beautiful or that touch us, inspiring us to overcome desperation, pain, and suffering for you who have this work or hear those words today. Let's all come together in this dance of strength and new beginnings. I also like butterflies, those little insects whose lives are whole of worthiness without words.

Through these pages, you were my muse, word picture, and teacher of those transformations. Finally, we back over life's dynamic strength

– anonymous and often overlooked yet constantly moving us through. For the breath that lives on and for the spirit that lifts high, I can never repay where endless beauty touches only to stir men's thankfulness.

As my pen touches everything on this long path of creation, these ideas and words I shared with everyone linger. It made this expedition possible and celebrates the unending cycle of people, their transformations, and the lovely things they hold dear: thank you, both seen and unseen.

I would not have thanked everyone properly if I didn't talk about hope. It may be hard to see or touch, but it is there and has helped even in the worst times by bringing light into dark moments. In the same way that every butterfly begins as a possibility waiting on the edge of the unrealized, hope has been the wings upon which this book was written.

From the depths of my transformed heart, I thank you. Your part in this journey will be forever woven into the decorative wings of this endeavor. Just as the butterfly leaves beauty wherever it lands, may this book leave traces of resilience, transformation, hope, and beauty in your lives.

Table of Contents

Introduction

In this world of living creatures, a butterfly is a unique specie that inspires us via its symbolic illustration of freedom, and profound transformation from the stage of caterpillar. Much like a butterfly grows from level to level, in addition, it indicates us that we too grow throughout our lifetime and end up something distinct. The transformation procedure of a caterpillar right into a butterfly affords a beautiful story that could inspire you to gracefully be given the fast modifications that may show up for your existence. As these pages flutter past, anticipate now not handiest to find the profound parallels between those winged wonders and the human spirit, however, to internalize a harbinger of hope: The ache that one has to endure due to a trade can help in spotting ones' authentic self, and from there you possibly can simplest go to develop towards a very lovely lifestyles.

Brief Overview of the Butterfly as a Symbol of Transformation and Freedom

The Long appreciated as a symbol of transformation—a sign of universal renewal, freedom, and change—the butterfly with its delicate wings gracefully flying—We delve into the profound symbolism of this delicate creature, etching an image that resonates deeply within the human spirit. The chapter presented here reveals the similarities between the life cycle of a butterfly and the metamorphosis of human migration.

Inside the limits of a chrysalis, the caterpillar dismantles, changing totally to rise as a butterfly. This metamorphosis stands as a potent allegory for moments in which life disassembles the familiar, nudging us towards renewal. Reflection upon these parallel stirs the soul, fostering a collective nod to the promise that lies within transformation, even when it arrives wrapped in the guise of trials and tribulations.

Butterflies connote freedom—flitting from blossom to blossom they manifest a dance that captures the essence of living unbound. It's a freedom earned through change, a testament to the courage required when one breaks the shells that once housed them. We find solace in this symbolism, a gentle reminder that freedom, often birthed through struggle, is an inherent part of our nature, waiting to unfurl with the right measure of time and persistence.

Each wingbeat of a butterfly signifies the resilience required to face the winds of adversity. It teaches us that within life's cyclones, there exists the potential to glide into winds of change, gaining steadiness and strength. Just as a storm offers the butterfly the power to ascend to remarkable heights, life's challenges are the gusts shaping our character, compelling our ascent to new viewpoints, charged with breathtaking vistas upon their conquest.

In its quiet beauty, the butterfly whispers of endurance, of survival through the most unexpected and remarkable transformation. Its life cycle, a series of transitions—weaving from vulnerability to magnificence—parallels the human experience, suggesting that within the threads of undergoing hardship, new beginnings are crafted. Thus, we weave our narratives, finding beauty in our struggles, knitting wounds into testimonies of survival and growth.

Imagine, if you will, the exquisite patience required of the butterfly as it awaits the fortitude to burst forth into the world again. Patience is a virtue the butterfly imparts without preaching, a virtue that is indispensable in our personal quests for reformation. To observe the butterfly is to learn the subtleties of patience, which, in turn, can become the scaffolding for our freedom and authenticity.

The lesson of the butterfly does not conclude with the newfound flight. It extends to the very nature of its journey—the ceaseless moving forward, the flutter towards an unseen destination. Our own journeys too are a seamless foray into the new, with hidden bends and shadows that unfold only upon approach, making the insight of the butterfly's travels a beacon for continuity against the backdrop of life's constants and variables.

In its silence, the butterfly also teaches us of the inner strength that possibilities hold—the strength to push through confinements, seeking the light of day and the kiss of the sun. Strength isn't always the roar; sometimes, it's the gentle unfolding of wings dried under the warmth of new beginnings, readying themselves for the maiden flight—the journey to which we are all destined, the flight towards liberation.

The luminosity on a butterfly's wings serves not simply to shock the spectator but to remind each of us that from obscurity can rise dynamic color and light. Within the center of life's grayscale, there are multicolored minutes of excellence. It's an understanding that excellence isn't a state of being, but the result of getting there, staying with it, and winning within the conclusion.

Let us not overlook the butterfly's flexibility and adaptability, an insightful nod to the mutable nature of existence. The butterfly's capacity to yield and respond to the environment without forsaking its essence captures the balance between being and becoming. Taking note, we can embrace our environment's challenges as fluid, modifying without losing our core being, just as the butterfly dips and dives but always remains, at its heart, a creature of exquisite transformation.

To the attentive eye, the butterfly too envoys the significance of the moment—each brief landing on a blossom, a delay within the amazing exhibition of its life. It highlights the esteem of the display, the presently, where freedom is really experienced—not within the yesterdays nor the tomorrows, but within the abundance and completion of what is, here and presently. Hence, the butterfly inclinations us to savor each minute, for each bears the weight and intelligence of freedom's story.

Butterflies teach us to embrace the lightness of being as well—a quality often obscured by life's burdens. As it effortlessly rides the zephyrs, the butterfly models a life unburdened, a call to shed the heavy cloaks we don ourselves, whether they are of doubt, fear, or despondence. Its flight, an invitation to lift our gazes and hearts, aspiring to fly high, to soar with purpose and delight across the canvasses of our lives.

One could say the butterfly's journey is a profoundly solitary one, yet it unfolds within the canopies of interconnected ecosystems. Such a parallel to our human experiences cannot be ignored. Our transformations, though deeply personal, resonate and reverberate across the web of lives we touch. The freedom we seek and may achieve is not just our own but contributes to a collective unfolding, a shared tapestry of emancipation and growth.

At this point, it would be notable that the butterfly educates us that the core of opportunity lies inside our own cocooned hearts. It's a clarion call to unfurl our wings, grasp our true selves, and discharge the away potential that lies torpid inside. This respectable creature's move through life serves as a symbol for our capacity for alter, versatility, and the unstoppable soul that characterizes the journey for individual flexibility.

As this exploration unfolds, we will carry with us the essence of the butterfly—observing, learning, and applying its lessons of transformation and freedom to our lives. We will trace its flight through the chapters of growth, resilience, renewal, and the fulfillment that comes forth when one truly spreads their wings to embrace their path—irrespective of the thunderstorms, winds, or stillness they may encounter.

Chapter 1:
The Metaphorical Exploration of the Butterfly's Life Cycle as a Guide to Personal Growth and Happiness

As time unfolds and pages turn, we often seek stories that resonate to the core of our being. Nature, in its puzzling and wondrous ways, holds a reflect to the human soul, none more exquisitely than the butterfly—a animal that has captivated the human creative energy for ages, symbolizing change, opportunity, and the potential that lies torpid inside us all.

Here it is as though we are on a transformative journey that draws upon the ethereal lifecycle of the butterfly to clarify the pathways toward individual development and joy. For, within the delicate wings of this wonderful animal, there lies a significant metaphor—one that talks of persevering battles, grasping alter, and eventually, the spreading out of magnificence borne from difficulty.

It is within the delicate balance of nature's hand that we begin to understand the intricate stages of metamorphosis. Just as the butterfly must navigate through its own phases of spectacular rebirth, so do we as individuals confront the various seasons of our lives, the moments of hardship and flowering jubilation that sculpt our existence.

Envision for a minute the caterpillar, whose modest shape gives a false representation of the enchantment it harbors. Isn't it associated to our own latent potential? Our journey, just like the caterpillar's, frequently begins with a humble, terrestrial beginning, however inside us are the seeds of grand change, anticipating the fertile moments that welcome us to bloom.

Experiencing the state of cocoon requires surrender, a readiness to be enveloped by the unknown. Within the limits of the chrysalis, a transformation brews—a speculative chemistry that can be compared to the individual reflection and challenges we confront, and which hold the keys to our significant advancement.

Within the quietude and solitude of the cocoon phase, there is a poignant narrative of growth. This is where our previous understandings and former selves can be reshaped, redefined, reimagined. And just as the butterfly does not emerge prematurely, we too must cultivate patience in the quiet unraveling of our own becoming.

Think of the apparently unfavorably exertion it takes for the butterfly to break free from its chrysalis, the battle that fortifies its wings for the looming travel. In our lives, such struggles are not to be feared but embraced, as they fortify our spirit and prepare us for the flights ahead.

Yet is not beauty itself born from struggle? The butterfly, with its striking tones and smooth balance, does not just exist; it captivates, motivates, reminding us that out of difficulty develops a magnificence that's not simply visual, but intrinsic—a flexibility that we as well have, prepared to spread out its wings inside us.

How can we not marvel at the transformation from a grounded being to one that defies gravity, taking to the skies with apparent ease and tranquility? Our own lives are much the same, filled with boundless opportunities to rise above and find our own currents of air upon which to soar.

The resilience is not just in the act of flying, but in the preparation for it—the nurturing courage and commitment that precedes flight. Just as the butterfly must weather storms and winds, we too must build the tenacity to navigate our storms, finding strength in the very act of enduring.

As the butterfly hops from blossom to bloom, it shares within the move of life, contributing to the cycle of development and recovery. Such is our call to spread joy, to foster connections, and to be agents of positivity and change within our own lives and in the lives of others.

With each flutter of a butterfly's wings, there is an unspoken narrative of freedom, a dance along the delicate edges of the possible and the manifest. What if we too approached life with this same sense of boundless curiosity and liberation? Could we not rewrite the symphonies of our days with the melodious tunes of happiness?

So, let us cast our look upon the horizon, where the sky meets the guarantee of boundless potential, and let the life cycle of the butterfly direct us. Not just as an imaginable trait, but as a constant renewal of the magnificence and versatility in all of us.

As we share in this metaphorical exploration, the flutter of wings against the currents of life becomes a symphony, a resonant chord that weaves through the essence of being. Together, we journey through the transformative echoes of the butterfly's life cycle—a guide, a teacher, a beacon illuminating the path toward our own personal growth and the elation of true happiness.

Within the chapters that follows, we'll dig into each stage of this wondrous lifecycle, each chapter an investigation not just of the butterfly's natural development, but a parallel to our own opportunities for growth. Let us step into this investigation with open hearts and minds, prepared to grasp the significant parallels and lessons that awaits relative to the fragile movement of the butterfly's wings.

The Cocoon of Challenges

As we emerge from the introductory caress of transformation and freedom, Chapter One enfolds us in the gossamer threads of the *cocoon of challenges*. This intricate phase, where the butterfly within bristles against its silken prison, mirrors our own struggles as tightly as our second skin. Here, we delve into the heart of adversity, where each tightening bind is not a harbinger of entrapment, but a vital whisper of impending blossoming. We explore the cocoon as a crucible instead of a tomb, forging the fortitude needed to emerge grander and stronger. Herein lies not just a story but the resilience of the human spirit in trials and tribulations representing the truth that only through tested minds could the wings to man's full potential be unfurled. In this cocoon, it whispers of the potential to transform such hidden softness into visceral splendor and power.

Drawing Parallels Between Life Struggles and the Cocoon Stage in a Butterfly's Life

Challenges envelop us much like a cocoon grips the form of the future butterfly. Obscured and constrained, this stage is neither the beginning nor the end but a necessary transition that shapes the essence of what is to come. Much like the eventual butterfly, individuals face their own periods of enclosure, where growth, though hidden from view, churns with fervent intensity.

In this protective embrace, there lies a profound paradox. It is within the bind of the cocoon — a space that some may view as a confinement — that the caterpillar is, in reality, liberated. It can embody its potential, transforming into an entity far more remarkable than its former self. So too, humans discover in their deepest adversities the potential for extraordinary transformation.

The cocoon demands patience and perseverance. There's an inherent understanding that the process cannot be rushed; similarly, the arduous ordeals of life require a quiet strength and stoic endurance. One can't simply escape the struggles but must move through them, transforming pain into power, much like the caterpillar metamorphoses into a creature of the air.

The tight enclosure of the cocoon may represent the pressures of life that constrict us — loss, failure, or rejection. Yet, just as the caterpillar uses this time to develop wings, so too can individuals harness these pressures to forge new strengths, passions, and a deeper understanding of their purpose.

Consider the act of emerging from the cocoon. It is not a mere shedding of walls but an active struggle vital to survival. Without this struggle, the butterfly's wings would fail to gain the strength required to fly. In every hardship faced, there is an equivalent necessity. The barriers we push through fortify us, preparing us for the flights we are yet to take.

The isolation of the cocoon doesn't signify a departure from the world but suggests a deep inward journey. It dissolves to some extent in the chrysalis, to be reborn, quite literally, as it were. So, in quiet recesses of our challenges, we too may feel dissolved, disintegrated underneath the weight of proceedings. Yet from this apparent undoing emerges a clearer self, alive and new.

Change within the cocoon is not visible to the outside world, and often, personal transformation is just as discreet. The work done in the soul's hidden chambers frequently goes unnoticed by others, yet it is no less potent. Each quiet victory over adversity is a victory, nonetheless, laying the foundation for a life of grace and tenacity.

Where the caterpillar saw the end, the butterfly sees the beginning. Likewise, what is often mistaken for a conclusion in human experience is frequently an inauguration. The moments of our deepest doubts coincide with the first flutters of possibility, the prelude to a more illumined existence.

It's important to note that not all cocoons bear the test of time and struggle. Some are breached prematurely or meet untimely ends. Our own paths too can be marked by shared failures and false starts. Yet, even in these broken efforts, there lie invaluable lessons and the seeds of determined future endeavors.

The beauty of this stage is that it becomes both the retreat and construction site. The caterpillar knows intuitively when to weave its cocoon and lay back, just as sometimes we know intuitively when its time to step back, reflect and regroup before emerging brighter and more magnificent.

Adversity in this light is an intricately woven cocoon — a metamorphosing event, a personal epoch marked by intense refinement and discovery. The confinements we face in life are not mere hindrances, but opportunities dressed in disguise, calling forth courage and evoking a latent power within.

The darkness of the cocoon, an inky envelope, is the backdrop against which the luminosity of change is most starkly and beautifully rendered. It is the shadow that defines the light. And in our lives, it is the depth of our struggles which amplify the brilliance of our triumphs.

In surrender to the process, the butterfly entrusts itself to the transformation, never doubting its outcome. Humans, too, must cultivate a measure of faith as they endure their own metaphorical cocoons. The assurance that the dark and pressing present is but the precursor to an emerging future, replete with color and flight, can be a wellspring of hope.

The cocoon stage, a vital interlude, teaches the importance of embracing the entirety of life's cycle. We learn not only to withstand the trials but to delve into their core, to seek and find growth, to acknowledge that within every limitation lies the kernel of unbounded possibility.

As the butterfly finally slips free, wings damp and crumpled, it is not the end but an exquisite commencement. Life's struggles, in their parallel manner, give way to fresh starts, unexplored horizons, and the irreplaceable joy found in the first flutter of newfound wings. Within the cocoon of challenges lies the profound transformation, from which one can emerge not just unscathed, but reborn, soaring on the resilient wings of hard-earned wisdom and beauty.

Encouraging Readers to Embrace Challenges as Opportunities for Growth

As the last chapter closed its final page, we found ourselves enveloped in the symbolism of the cocoon, understanding its significance in our own lives. But to truly internalize this lesson, consider how we might encourage ourselves to embrace challenges not as barriers but as the very soil in which our potential can take root and flourish.

Imagine a moment in the transformation of the world of the caterpillar within the scant boundaries of its house of silk. Does it tremble at the darkness? Does it struggle against the lacing that encases it? Or might it understand, through intuition deep as the roots of ancient trees, that this darkness is not an end but a profound transformation? Within this enigma lies the key, urging us to see our challenges as caterpillars do—a prelude to metamorphosis.

Now, reflect on a time in your life when the walls closed in, heavy and insurmountable. What if, at that moment, you had known that within struggle lies the seeds of growth? The narrative we construct around our hardships can cause us to wilt or flourish. To embrace challenge is to rewrite that narrative, to see struggles as the cocoon, temporary yet essential, in the unfolding story of who we are becoming.

Challenges are a language of their own, steeped in the harsh yet nurturing tongues of life. They communicate truths through adversity, each problem resonant with the opportunity for learning and expansion. The cocoon doesn't speak to the caterpillar of limitation; it whispers of the wings it's yet to unfold. And so, our challenges whisper to us—if only we listen—of the strengths we're yet to discover.

During the most violent storms we discover the level of resilience we never knew we had. And as the storms gather on the horizon, instead of reeling back and preparing to be destroyed, consider that we instead might be preparing our sails for a journey that will blow us all away and just might tell just exactly what kind of stuff we're made of.

In truth, the most awe-inspiring achievements often sprout from the soil of great difficulty. Each mountain summited begins with treacherous paths and every flourishing business once faced looming risk. Accepting challenges as opportunities is akin to recognizing that within every acorn lies the majesty of an oak. The might within each of us is no less boundless.

Recognize that this acceptance does not mute the struggle, does not diminish the pain of the moment. Indeed, the sharp edges of hardship cut deeply, and to deny this would be to deny the very truth of our humanity. But through acceptance, we might also perceive the sharpening of our spirit, as the oyster embraces the irritation that will cultivate its pearl.

For when we open our hearts to challenge, we as well unlock the potential for unimaginable fulfillment. Growth should not be measured in the absence of pain, but rather in ability to move through it, to let it shape us while we remain undefeated by its weight. But as they say the greatest tales and ballads sing not of lives untouched by strife but of those that faced the night and heralded the dawn.

This is a journey of embracing the challenges with patience. Such transformation doesn't take place in an instant, but it has to process and facilitate unfoldment. We come comfort step by step in our ability to endure and into that endurance is woven the tapestry of our personal legends. Patience is unwavering in belief in fruition of our becoming.

We should also allow for the art of surrender in order to embrace challenges. In this metamorphosis, there is the art of letting go – it is a releasing that which was to make space for what will be. Just as the butterfly cannot emerge until the caterpillar cease to be, so also, we will not emerge from holding onto the identity shaped by our past struggles in order that we may embrace our future self.

Within this practice of release is the joy of self-discovery. For as we shed the layers that once defined us, we uncover new facets of our character, gleaming and untested. The discovery of self is not a destination, but a journey marked by the waypoints of our challenges.

Do not mistake this encouragement as a call to go in search of hardship, but rather to rise with grace when it finds you. Life, unbidden, will provide its share of trials, each an opportunity to cultivate the virtues that define the content of our character. The hero's journey is not in the seeking of trouble, but in answering the call when it arrives at your door.

To grow through challenges is to accept their inevitability. It is the same understanding that leads the butterfly to trust in the integrity of its wings—the knowledge that they were built through the struggle of emergence. Trust in your own strength, and in the growth that lies concealed within every obstacle you face.

It is, therefore, for us to venture out into the wilderness of this unknown, secure in the knowledge that our deepest selves' momentum awaits us. For as the butterfly, changed, wings to the skies so shall we rise fueled by the unseen strength of all our yesterdays. Embrace the cocoon, for it is the first step toward the boundless expanses of the skies.

Remember that the caterpillar endures the darkness for the exultations of flight. May we also come out with wings unfolded ready to take off in the winds of development and opportunities that is awaiting us in the bright sun of life's undying day.

Personal Anecdotes and Stories Illustrating Resilience During Difficult Times

In the still struggle, there is a whisper of resilience fiercely echoed down chambers of human spirit. These are but anecdotes of those whispers turned into a chorus of survival, stories delicate spun from the silk of human challenges.

There's the tale of Jonas, whose life, much like a cocoon, was tightly wound by the twine of adversity. A man of modest means, he found himself in the throes of joblessness, the pavement beneath his feet seeming to crumble with every step. Yet, amid the countless rejections, his perseverance became his chrysalis. He honed his craft, wielded his skills with the finesse of an artisan, painting hope where despair once lingered. Over time, Jonas emerged triumphant, crafting a career mosaic from the shards of his persistence.

Ella's story sings a similar tune. Diagnosed with a chronic illness, she faced mornings where her body whispered surrender. Yet her resilience roared louder. Day after day, Ella chose to find beauty in her pain, alchemizing her suffering into a canvas of inspiration. It was in the smallest of activities that she found her greatest victories—

painting, writing, breathing in the world when it seemed to compress around her.

Then there are those like Liam, a soldier of life's arbitrary battles. A beacon for his family, he withstood the gale of grief following the loss of a beloved. The days muddled into nights, yet he discovered solace in the pulse of the natural world. In tending to his garden, planting seeds, he nurtured not just flora but the tender seedlings of healing within his soul. His hands, though calloused, wove threads of continuity between his heart and the earth.

Consider Maya, whose entrepreneurial dreams crumbled beneath economic strain. Her aspirations, once vivid as a monarch's wings, seemed to dull against the gray of uncertainty. Yet, she pushed forth, her spirit never yielding to despair. She learned, adapted, and reinvented her business, breathing life into it as one would to a dwindling flame. Her efforts blossomed, and in time, she flew on the winds of a success born from the ashes of failure.

Stories like these echoes in the lives of so many. Take Sarah, a young talent in a sprawling metropolis, watching as the lights dimmed on Broadway. Her stage—the realm where she came alive—fell dark amidst the pandemic. Yet, within her confined apartment, Sarah danced, sang, and acted, forging a digital stage that reached across isolate miles, touching hearts tethered by shared human experience.

Zachary's resolve was tested by addiction, a tempest that churned within him, threatening to engulf his very being. The road to sobriety was fraught with relapse's cruel cliff edges. Yet Zachary's mettle became the thermometer setting his destination, forward to a life of clarity and purpose. Every day became a testament to his strength, every second in sobriety a milestone on his odyssey of self-discovery.

And who could ignore Lauren, the teacher who saw the walls of her classroom dissolve into virtual space? Tasked with reaching out to her students across the digital divide, she became an innovator overnight. Her resilience transformed her approach, leveraging the power of storytelling and creative platforms to ignite curiosity in young minds around the globe.

Jackson's resilience shone in the face of discriminatory currents. Facing the harsh tides of injustice, he lifted his voice, becoming a beacon for those sightless to the spectrum of humanity's hues. With every peaceful march, with every word he carved into the fabric of society, he stitched a legacy of equality and hope.

As a single mother, kept her own ledger and balanced every inch of life with better precision than an accountant. She led between roles like a ballet dancer between poses for there was no sense in making those closest to her suffer her self-righteous mutiny. Finding strength in the silent hours, weaving love into the fabric of their lives, resilience to show them that it wasn't simply about surviving it meant flourishing.

Amidst the chaos of natural disaster, Miguel stood firmly rooted. With winds that threatened to steal everything he held dear; he became a calm within the storm. It was the foundation of a collective rebirth, in indisputable testimony to the human indomitable spirit and powerful unity that was rebuilding the community brick by brick.

In the realm of discovery, Nadia's tale of resilience glimmers. A scientist on the verge of breakthroughs, she met failure as if an old friend, learning from each misstep. Her gaze remained fixed on the horizon of possibility, unblinking in the face of experimentation's relentless tests. Her tenacity became a lighthouse, guiding her to shores of innovation and progress.

Ben, a musician, felt the strangle of silence as concert halls turned hollow. Yet, his music did not fade into the background. He played from his balcony, notes cascading down the cityscape, offering symphonies of solidarity to his neighbors. Resilience, for Ben, was in the continuity of his craft, in the shared language of melodies that knew no border.

And so flows the river of resilience, with countless other streams branching from it. Abigail, who braved the stigma of mental health challenges, speaking openly and advocating fiercely. Mark, who turned his layoff into an opportunity for learning, coding his way into a new career trajectory. These are the tendons of human fortitude, the stories stirring within the cocoon of challenges.

Just as the butterfly wrestles in the darkness before it can fly, so too do human beings grapple with their trials. In the confinement of their cocoons, they find the essence of their resilience, and from their struggles, they emerge not broken but beautifully transformed. This tapestry of personal tales intricately interwoven reminds one of the inherent strengths within, waiting to unfurl into spectacular wings at dawn's first light.

Chapter 2:
Embracing Change

In the seamless weave of existence, it is the thread of change that tightens the fabric of our lives, urging us onward from the familiar cocoon of our reality. It lies in the heart of transformation discomfort —a fiery companion to growth very much akin to the metamorphosis from the caterpillar unto the butterfly. It is within this natural alchemy where the essence of personal development initiates; we find ourselves coiled therein the chrysalis of our own becoming.

. Adapting to change asks of us a certain yielding, a resilience nuanced with vulnerability as we unfold into new forms of strength. With practicality at its core, this chapter delves into the tumultuous yet rewarding process of embracing change. It is not intended to shelter you from the winds of change but to provide you tools to enable steering of your sails for being able to navigate into uncharted waters wisely. Is the dance of transformation not a most profound reflection of our own lives? It is an invitation to enter the boundless potential of what might be by passing through the gateway of the past. For in every moment of transition, there lies a breathtaking possibility: to emerge anew, wings wide, ready to fly.

Exploring the Metamorphosis Phase and Its Significance in Personal Development

As nature gently unwraps a new chapter in the life of the butterfly, so too, must we unfurl the parchment of our beings to reveal the poetry of transformation within us. The transformation stage, that lovely sequence of a caterpillar's change into a butterfly, is an odyssey of significant evolution akin to those minutes in our lives when we stand at the slope of who we were and look in ponder at who we should be or become.

In the heart of this transformation lies discomfort, a challenging but necessary companion on the journey to the embodiment of potential. The cocoon, a silken cradle of evolution, does not yield its treasure lightly. It requires of its inhabitant a total surrender to the unknown, a trust in the process that must seem unfathomable from the perspective of the caterpillar.

Personal development mirrors this process, demanding of us a similar trust, a dive into the depths of self that can bring with it both fear and exhilaration. Embracing change is not merely an act of acceptance, but an art of engagement with the forces that mold us into our next form. The metamorphosis phase teaches us the fundamental truth that growth is not passive—it is an act of creation, and we are both the artist and the clay.

Our wants to new statures are frequently laced with the deep-rooted need to shed the layers of our old selves. The caterpillar does not get to be a butterfly by accumulatively maintaining its old self but by disposing of it completely, developing anew without the limits of its previous being. This is the sigil of personal development—the conscious act of letting go, piece by piece, of what no longer serves us.

The journey within the chrysalis is silent and unseen. So too, our most transformative experiences often transpire in solitude, away from the eyes of the world. Alone with ourselves, we conquer our fears, escape our doubts, and become familiar to the language of our truest selves. It is here, in the stillness that precedes rebirth, that we gather the strength to face our own unveiling.

Metamorphosis is marked, too, by a period of vulnerability, of existing between states, neither caterpillar nor butterfly. We must honor this in-between space where we are raw and unformed, as it is the forge of our new identity. Just as butterflies must battle to free self from its chrysalis in order to reinforce its wings, so also we as well should wrestle with our impediments to discover our strength.

But what 's the import behind all this transformation, this upheaval and rebirth? It is in getting to be a greater, more refined adaptation of ourselves that we discover the key that opens the boundless spaces of our full potential. The emergence of the butterfly is confirmation to the power of resilience, lighting the way for each of our ways of discovering ourselves.

As one phase of life dissolves to make room for another, we encounter the promise of new horizons. The metamorphosis phase urges us to stretch beyond our familiar confines, to embrace the vastness of our possible futures. Personal development is not simply a transformation of what we do or how we think, but a profound alteration of our very spirits.

It is fundamental, then, to recognize the transformation stage not as an end but as a transition. With each phase of shedding of our skin, we are not essentially disposing of who we were, but also sharpening who we are getting to be. Each encounter, each battle, each leap into the obscure could be a brushstroke on the canvas of our lives.

Consider the butterfly's first flight, a testament to the value of persistence through uncertainty. Our initial steps into the changed self can be as tentative as that first flutter of wings, yet they signal the birth of a new journey, an exploration not just of the world but of the self within it.

Our lives are packed with moments that calls for an evolution— the conclusion of a relationship, the starting of another career, the quiet inner realization that we can no-more tread the same path of life but find a change. In these moments, the metamorphosis phase whispers to us that there is beauty in the courage it takes to unfurl our wings against the unknown.

This phase finds its worth in the acknowledgment that change is an integral part of the human experience. It celebrates the fact that we are malleable, capable of profound shifts in direction and purpose. As the butterfly develops from its temporal tomb, so can we rise from our self-imposed restrictions, lolling within the light of unused conceivable outcomes.

In the metamorphosis phase, we find the allegory for our deepest transformations, for the enduring truths that to change is to live, to struggle is to grow, and to emerge is to triumph. Embracing this dynamic cycle of change is to align ourselves with the rhythm of existence, to dance to the song of life that empowers every creature to become more than it was.

And so, in exploring the metamorphosis phase, we delve into the very essence of personal development. We unearth the significance of our own transitions, the shifts in our identities that shape our tomorrows. The transformation stage, at that point, isn't fairly a stage in a life cycle, but the exceptional pulse of a transformative existence— a signal that inside the strands of our being lies the potential for boundless rebirth.

Let us at this point take from the butterfly not just motivation but a guide, one that shows us the way towards grasping our transformation with elegance, with desire, and with an unyielding conviction within the potential that lies inside us all. It is in this stage that we discover our wings and learn to take off.

Discussing the Discomfort of Change and How It Leads to Positive Transformation

Change grasps us with an uncomfortable fervor, similar to the resolute squeeze of a cocoon around a soon-to-be butterfly. An encasement that is at once protection and prison. It is in this constriction, this unsettling shift from one form to another, that the magic of transformation begins – an agitation necessary for growth, pushing us toward a grand unveiling of potential. But the path is discomforting and it is this very unease that signals the breakthroughs ahead.

Imagine the caterpillar's final days before its metamorphosis. The once voracious feeder must now surrender to a relentless stillness, encased within silken threads of its own making. For us, as human souls, the silken threads symbolize the comfort zones we spin, and the act of breaking through asks us to leave behind what we've known. It is an inherent human trait to resist this departure from familiarity, but herein lies the valuable essence of progression.

Enduring the inconvenience of change is associated to the method of molting – the casting off of an ancient exterior because of a new development. This is often not a matter of inactivity; it requires dynamic engagement with our rising selves. Grasping this discomfort, hence, gets to be a deliberate choice to grow, to advance, to rise more vigorously adjusted to the cacophony and ensemble of life.

Recognizing discomfort as a herald of growth shifts our perception – much as the caterpillar must innately trust in its transformation. We begin to embrace the constriction of our cocoons, knowing that the pressure we feel is sculpting us into more magnificent forms. We submit to the process, realizing that the old must be shed to welcome the new.

But how can one weather the cyclical storms of change? Perhaps reflecting upon our past can provide solace – recalling times of upheaval that, despite initial resistance, brought us to greener pastures. These memories become beacons of hope, lamps illuminating the path to resilience and underscoring our capacity for reinvention.

Changes never really asks our permission; it comes rolling in without warning, asserting itself much like the sudden change of the wind's direction. One may find themselves flailing-about full of anxiousness at the loss of control. But as the larvae innately prepare for their metamorphoses, we too can arm ourselves with strategies: seeking support, committing to self-care, and practicing mindfulness, ensuring we're nurtured throughout our transformations.

Let us not forget that the threshold of transformation is lined with uncertainty. It tempts us with the potential of retreating to our old ways, our previous selves. But beyond this precipice lies the untamed beauty of becoming. As a caterpillar relinquishes its form to become a creature of the sky, we too are capable of astounding rebirths, each discomfort navigated a step toward our own soaring flight.

It is in metamorphosis that we discover a latent power hitherto untapped. Change requires adaptation – polishing of capabilities, acquisition of new knowledge, unceasing drive for self-improvement. Through that prism change was not an adversary, but a formidable teacher, a relentless architect redesigning the structures of our existence. However, the power of transformation usually comes at a cost of leaving the old self behind - which is usually ridden with grief, nostalgia, and pains.

The beauty of transformation, much like the splendor of a butterfly, lies in the acceptance of this loss as a necessary precursor to the gain. Mourning what was becomes part of our journey, enriching the tapestry of who we become.

With such a profound transformation from crawling to flying, the butterfly has some vulnerability. Once out, it cannot immediately make the flight of its life because first it must wait for wings to dry before taking first flight into the world. In the same vain, we too must allow us the grace of pausing, of owning up our transparent wings before setting out into the world afresh.

In this waiting, there is a silent fortitude – for the wings of change, though fragile at first, will soon empower us to ascend to new heights. We learn to become patient and trust on our own unfolding that every one of us is onto this journey of becoming.

We continue through stages of our change cacophony will transform into harmony.

What was once dissonant becomes a chorus of promise. We learn not just to endure change, but to dance with it, to wield it as a force of personal evolution and profound creativity.

And so, within the context of our lives, we must recognize that the journey through the discomfort of change is not a detour but the very road to our transformation. We are not bystanders to our metamorphosis, but its active participants – cocoon weavers, wing testers, sky chasers. There's no radical change without its discomforts as there is no growth without the pains of birthing a new self.

We, therefore, pursue in the knowledge that these pains are the prelude to the symphony of our tomorrow. It is without doubt this rite of passage that shapes us, defines us to be contestants of life and eventually frees us. To resist change is to squander the potential of our own wings. We must choose instead to embrace it, to allow its discomfort to shape us into the most authentic, vibrant versions of ourselves.

In closing this contemplation, we affirm the transformation awaiting us within our own chrysalises of change. For in the heart of discomfort lies a powerful truth: that we are perpetually evolving, and through this evolution, we discover the bliss of flight – a life lived with purpose, resilience, and unfettered joy. We vowed always to come out on the other side even more beautiful of spirit, stronger in faith, and sensitive to the wonders of God as captured in the beauties of our limitless skies and so visionary in each season of our lives that yet lay ahead.

Providing Practical Tips on Adapting to Change and Finding Strength in Vulnerability

Adaptability is the compass on this ever evolving path where change reigns king and queen. There is an indescribable beauty to be found in letting go and being changed by the new, but if there's one thing, we can learn from a butterfly it's that it forces itself to leave what used to be before it actually turns into something.

The first step towards adapting to change is to acknowledge it. Like the chrysalis stage of our winged exemplar, change often encases us in a swirl of uncertainty. Here, acceptance does not imply passive resignation, but rather a recognition of reality. Embrace the fact that change is upon you; this will ease the discomfort of the unknown.

Then, remember that just as the tissues of a caterpillar rearrange to allow birth of a butterfly, so must we let go or change the old aspects of ourselves to make room for new development. Determine what habits, convictions, or interpersonal connections no longer benefit you, and then gently let them go.

Lean into the discomfort. The chrysalis is constricted, there's no room for the creature within to avoid transformation. Understand that discomfort is not an enemy; that we should reframe it by thinking for it as a signpost towards new beginnings. It could be as of preparation, preparing you for a breadth of life ahead.

And develop patience, too. The metamorphosis doesn't happen in a single moment; it is a process. There may be backtracks, but they aren't the end. They are part of the sculpting work of life, chipping away what is superfluous, refining us for flight. Setbacks may occur, but they are not the end. They are part of the sculpting work of life, chipping away at what is superfluous, refining us for flight.

While adapting, seek perspective. Sometimes, our sight is limited to the confines of the cocoon. Step back and attempt to view change through a wider lens. It may be a path leading toward a more fulfilling direction or an opportunity to grow in ways previously unimagined.

Remember, vulnerability is not weakness but it's a profound strength. The very prospect of opening ourselves to the uncertainties which lie in wait of us in the future, can be every bit as intimidating as facing the world for the first time with those fragile wings showing the extent of resilience.

To find strength in vulnerability, it is crucial to cultivate a support network. Reach out to friends, family, or trusted advisors who can buoy you in moments when doubt seeps in. This web of connections can anchor us and remind us that we are not alone in our journeys.

Practice self-care. The transformational process can be taxing on both the body and spirit. Give yourself permission to rest, to nurture your wellbeing with activities that rejuvenate you—just as a chrysalis needs its time to develop in peace.

Set small, achievable goals. Change can seem less daunting when broken down into manageable steps. Each small victory is a confidence builder, reinforcing your ability to navigate through the shifts in your environment.

Develop adaptability by stepping outside of your comfort zone regularly. Much like the caterpillar must surrender the only world it's known, we too must explore new frontiers. Challenge yourself with new experiences and dabble in the unfamiliar with curiosity.

Embrace continuous learning. The world inside the chrysalis changes, so do the perceptions about the world outside. Look for a new knowledge, which is going to be an instrument in honing the adaptation capabilities as well as armor toward any changes that comes along.

Maintain a journal of your transformation. Just as scientists log the stages of a butterfly's metamorphosis, keep track of your journey through change. Reflecting on your thoughts and progress can provide clarity and reinforce the positives of your evolution.

Lastly, affirm your journey. Speak gently with yourself and encourage yourself to know that indeed it requires courage for the embrace of change. Affirmations strengthen our belief in self and support us in the journey of being agents of our own self-change.

In the garden of life, change is that very soil that our next selves must spring from. It's not about surviving change but thriving through it. For, as the butterfly shows, to be vulnerable is to let in some of the beauty of living—a dance with the winds of change that if one leans into leads to a life of vivid

Chapter 3:
The Beauty in Adversity

Having wrapped ourselves in the embrace of transformation and navigated the discomfort of our ever-changing selves, we arrive at an inflection point where the seemingly insurmountable pressures grant us a paradoxical gift. In the life cycle of a butterfly, adversity isn't merely a phase; it is the chisel that sculpts the breathtaking vibrancy from a once earthbound creature. Much like the struggles that dampen our spirit—yet serve to sharpen our resolve—this chapter unveils a tapestry woven from the threads of human resilience. Here, we'll uncover those tales that illuminate the exquisite alchemy of the soul, where sorrows are transfigured into strength, where scars become symbols of beauty, and every tear shed waters the soil from which we emerge more majestic than we ever fathomed we could be.

The quaking earth below our feet and the storms that batter our wings do not signify an end but a beginning—a harbinger of an epoch wherein we, too, discover that within adversity lies the essence of our beauty, the growth of our character, and the true measure of our brilliance. In these shared stories, we'll delve into how challenges are not just endured but treasured, not merely survived but transformed into the very core of our personal splendor that outshines the night's darkest moments.

Deep beauty that can come from problems and hard times we go through in life. These paragraphs tell us to change our view on problems. It helps people find the power hidden inside bad times and tough situations. This makes them stronger from past troubles they had faced or are facing now at present day. Discovering the transforming force that is embedded inside moments of suffering and adversity is the goal of this chapter, which encourages readers to redefine their viewpoint on problems. In this article, we investigate the beauty of life's failures and how being strong enough to take on our own shortcomings helps us get back up.

The life cycle of a butterfly as a metaphor for changing our views on problems conveys the following lessons in ways, we can draw inspiration from the butterfly's life cycle to transform our perspectives:

1. Egg stage: At first, the butterfly puts its eggs on a plant. Just like that, if we have a problem, first thing to do is accept and admit it exists. This means realizing there's a problem and accepting the task of finding it answer.

2. Caterpillar stage: After being born, the caterpillar eats leaves. It grows really quickly. Likewise, to alter our opinion about troubles we need information and learn more knowledge on the matter. This might be about learning, asking for help or taking importance from past experiences that connect to the issue.

3. Chrysalis stage: The bug rolls up in a chrysalis, changing itself from inside out. Likewise, if we want to change how we see problems, it is important that we spend time thinking about ourselves deeply. We need to look closely at our ideas, unfair thoughts, and suppositions about the issue. This is about asking ourselves if our initial ideas are right and being ready to see things in a different way.

4. Metamorphosis stage: In the chrysalis, a big change happens to the caterpillar. When it's over, out comes a butterfly instead of just an ordinary buggy creature like we were used to before.

Likewise, we need to be open-minded and ready for a change in perspective on issues. This involves going through a life-changing process. This might need us to stop doing old behaviors, thinking wrongly or getting rid of views that are not helping anymore. It needs accepting new thoughts, different ways to handle problems and being ready for changes.

5. Butterfly stage: When the butterfly appears for first time, it shows a new way of looking at things. It looks at the world differently, with increased understanding and changed views. Just like that, when we look differently at issues, we get a new point of view. We become better at finding answers and stronger. We learn to change easier, think outside the box, and bounce back from problems. We learn to view problems as chances for growth and tackle them with hope and sticking power.

We can get inspiration from a butterfly's life cycle. This tells us that issues are not just stuck or too hard to solve. Instead, these are chances for everyone to grow and change personally.

Highlighting the Idea That Challenges Can Lead to Personal Beauty and Strength

From that cocoon, we look out towards the horizon and realize and unyielding freedom from which this truth provides – challenges hold the secret soil from which personal beauty and strengths sprout. It is in the churning tumult of life's trials, that measure our spirit and tend to cause refinement in our most exquisite qualities. To deny this is to deny the essence of all growth; to embrace it is to unfurl the wings of our fullest potential.

Imagine, if you will, the relentless labor of the butterfly as it pushes through the confines of its chrysalis. There is a raw persistence, an inherent struggle in breaking free from the bounds of its former self.

31

So too must we labor against the perimeters of our known world, pressing with all our might against the barriers cocooning what we may yet become. It's a formidable process, yet through the straining and stretching, our former limitations are cast aside, and our capacity for beauty is revealed.

Imagine the unremitting toil of the butterfly as it makes a way out of the prison of its cocoon. an inherent struggle in breaking free from the bounds of its former self. So too must we labor against the perimeters of our known world, pressing with all we might against the barrier's cocoons encase what we yet may become. It is a grisly process but from the straining and stretching, our former limitations are discarded, and our capacity for beauty is exposed.

The trials we encounter are as varied as the patterns on a butterfly's wings – loss, failure, heartbreak – yet they all share a common gift. They carve spaces within - chasms that can be filled with newfound wisdom, compassion, and resilience. It is in the wake of adversity where the reflection in the mirror begins to change - where we see someone stronger, wiser, more radiantly alive than before.

Find the Positive Side in Challenges

Pain and Struggle Have the Power to Transform: We often find personal growth during hard times. These tough situations help us discover what can make us better people. This part talks about a miraculous process to change the challenges life gives into persons for growth personally. As a reader in your journey, look at how hard times are like butterflies' shell stage. This has the power to change human characters and good feelings: even though it is difficult now, this may make you much better in future.

Personal growth gained when things are hard is a great and life-changing process that can make big changes in a person. When difficult things happen, we usually find powerful inside courage and durability that maybe we didn't know was there. These hard times can help us grow as people and cause magical change in ourselves.

1. Self-reflection and introspection: Tough times make us look at ourselves and study our views, opinions, and mindset. We have to ask ourselves about the decisions we make, why we do it and what actions are taken. By looking at ourselves and thinking deeply, we get to know more about who we are. We also discover what really matters most in our lives. This process helps us show where personal growth is needed and needs change.

2. Building resilience: Times of trouble always check how tough we can be. Hard times push us to do things we don't usually like, and they make us change, find answers, and keep on going. As we deal with these problems, slowly we start getting stronger. We learn how to come back and recover from bad things that happen. This is called resilience - the power of bouncing back after tough times. We get a new strength that helps us handle what is happening and it also readies us to deal with anything tough in the future. This becomes very important for our lives.

3. Expanding perspectives: Bad times often make us very narrow-minded. We start to just think about the nearest issue we're facing at that moment. But our personal growth comes when we can change how we look at things and see the whole story. We start to look at other ideas, check out various chances and accept new ways of thinking. This bigger way of thinking lets us get rid of thoughts that limit us. It also leads to new ideas and personal progress.

4. Emotional growth and empathy: Hard times can bring strong feelings like being scared, sad or mad. By going through these feelings, we learn more about our own emotions and grow in

being able to feel what others may feel if they are dealing with the same difficulties. This emotional growth helps us connect with others on a deeper level, be there for them and help make our communities better.

5. Strengthening relationships: Difficult times show the real connections between people. When we deal with challenges, it's friends and family who help us. We also build stronger bonds with them during tough times. These shared experiences make a feeling of togetherness, faith and common understanding. Times are hard. To grow in a personal way, learn to talk well with others and work on close relationships so that you stay connected even when things are tough.

During tough times, personal development makes us grow stronger and smarter. It helps create a better version of us that is more able to recover from difficulties. We learn to know ourselves better plus become more ready for change, and courageous. The amazing change can be seen in both what we do and how our actions act. It also shows inside on the way we think about life including rules, standards or normal ways of doing things that everyone agrees to follow: This is done traditionally through customs, ceremonies to show appreciation for cultural ideas passed down from old generations called traditions beliefs set out by people before us. We start to feel very thankful for the things we've learned from bad times and a deeper understanding of how strong we can be.

This growth lets us face coming problems with fresh, strong hope and belief. We start being more ready to think in various ways, adjustable and willing to find answers. The magic change is to go from being a person who perhaps didn't want or feared dealing with problems, into someone that sees difficulties as openings for improvement and change.

Moreover, growing through difficult times usually changes what we value and helps us decide better on life. We get a better knowledge of what is important to us, things we love and goals we want. So we can change our lives a lot, like look for new jobs or work places. We might want to focus on keeping healthy and not hurt ourselves too much. It's also good to care more about friendships that mean something special one of us these changes happen because of studying 200 years ago without jet airplanes yet it became travel further times took longer near impossible yesterday.

In the end, personal development can happen in tough times. It's a wonderful change that happens within someone. It needs you to think about yourself, build up your strength, get new ideas and feelings. It also helps with feeling emotions better and makes connections even stronger in life's journey. By changing this way, we get tougher people with more knowledge and strength. Then ready to handle life's problems feeling brave for the future.

Our narratives may be peppered with chapters of hardship, but each sentence builds upon the last, crafting a story of endurance and courage. Each struggle etches into us a greater ability to weather the storms yet to come and a more profound beauty that is not merely seen but felt. It is through this tempering process that we come to realize our true strength, hard-won and irrefutable.

It might sound like something that is not easily understood in an instinctive way but, oftentimes, it is only in the darkest of times that life's brilliance is most vivid. In the same way, a raw uncut gemstone's semi-delineated imperfections and fractures reflect the light at an unlimited number of new angles, to polish away any brilliance we may not come to consider. Adversity doesn't diminish us; it amplifies our essence – creating a multifaceted brilliance only forged under pressure.

Let us not forget, however, that this process is not without its pain.

But let's not forget that this process, is not without pain. Growth takes an unraveling, shedding of skins, and dissolution can bring raw exposure. However, just as the emerging butterfly must rest and let its wings dry, we too must allow ourselves the grace of such a pause, get healed and mix our newly revealed strength for full integration into who we are becoming.

We must acknowledge that the journey through adversity is a profoundly personal one. What brings one person to their knees may barely phase another. Yet there's a thread of universality in the experience - a shared understanding that true beauty and strength are often birthed through hardship. Embracing this truth allows us to bear witness to the full spectrum of our resilience and emerge not just intact but transformed.

Consider those quiet testimonies of others who have walked through the fires of life yet emerged with a splendor phoenix-like; people who wear their scars as badges of honor and humility. Their stories filled the annals of inspiration, teach us not that it isn't an absence of struggle that defines us but how we rise from it's ashes to reclaim our light.

To find beauty in adversity is to unearth the hidden treasures within our stories. It's a beauty that doesn't fade with time but deepens, a strength that becomes the bedrock of our existence. Our most painful memories is like a churned up soil on there we sow the seeds of a new chapter full in hope of growing.

The supernatural enablement of the human soul is hard at work, turning the outcomes from our trials into the character of gold that shines through. Our most grueling challenges often give rise to talents and strengths we were previously blind to, like flawless diamonds formed under life's unrelenting pressures.

Instead of letting the challenges that we faced hold us back, let us cling on the lessons that they have taught as we go forward. Weaving these fragile threads into our mental fabric will make unbreakable mosaic of resilience. Our rise from the darkness into the light is reflected in every thread.

When we reflect on the vibrant life of the butterfly, we are reminded that strength and beauty are not destinations but processes. They do not exist despite adversity but because of it. The very forces that seek to test our mettle are the same that polish us into beings of extraordinary mettle and grace.

Keep trusting in the transforming potential of your struggles as you navigate the colorful tapestry of life, with its inevitable peaks and troughs. As we take deep breaths and cautious steps ahead, let us make room for the power and beauty that we are nurturing. And in our heart of hearts, know that our challenges are merely the chrysalis from which we will emerge, not broken, but breathtakingly beautiful.

We are not merely created to survive, but to flourish, and it is in the face of hardship that we discover this unchanging fact. The fires of adversity that burn within us are like a tempering flame; they ignite a ferocity and beauty that may illuminate an entire room, motivate an entire generation, and shed light on the depths of our soul. Challenges may additionally shape us; however it is our reaction to them that in reality defines the contours of our splendor and the fortitude of our energy.

We can choose, then, to see our struggles now not as curses, however as crucibles wherein the full spectrum of our humanity is subtle. And in that desire lies the energy to transform our darkest hours into our greatest victories, our private sorrows into the most profound wellspring of our beauty and power.

Recognize the Power in Being Vulnerable.

Being vulnerable doesn't mean you are weak, instead it shows real strength to confront your own problems. We celebrate the courage needed for recognizing weakness or what this author called growth areas) it fosters the possibility of finding growth. It also shows how embracing vulnerability can lead one to build new power. Therefore, you are asked to behold the beauty in being open and think of it as power from the viewpoint of a butterfly's wings. Those wings may seem weak, but they can still be strong and not break easily, like our own hearts or minds if we let ourselves show vulnerability with others.

When the forgoing is properly understood, the subject can beat the challenges to growth as a person. It helps to take steps to progress for yourself, life experiences become relatable. There are known stories about people who found out a lot of good and growth during their own tough times. The stories are related in "Personal Stories of trouble turning into Beautiful endings." These yarns help to support us by putting forward examples that demonstrate even though life provides challenges internal shifts can take place. The success of people who changed their failures into big improvements makes readers feel better and encouraged. They can see themselves in the story as a sign of hope, inspiration or comfort that comes with it too! Their wins prove to everyone that even if you fail, there's still a chance to succeed after all!

Sharing Stories of Individuals Who Have Found Beauty in Their Own Adversities

In times of difficulty, the strength of human will is reflected. There are innumerable people whose life exemplify the beautiful transformation that takes place as butterflies emerge out from their cocoons ready to fly away. Those stories are about more than making it through tough times but growing into something bigger than themselves.

Think about Anna, a talented young artist whose autoimmune illness left her unable to use her hands. Anna discovered a new artistic medium when others sensed the end of their careers. Instead of her fingers, She learnt to use her writs to handle the brush, and as a result of that, her paintings became more energetic and full of life. . As evidence that beauty can emerge from adversity, her artwork is currently on display in museums and galleries. She overcame obstacles and now uses her talent and determination to paint a vibrant picture.

Or Leo, who, like a butterfly caught in an unexpected storm, endured the grief of losing a loved one. He turned his sorrow into the engine that drives a non-profit encouraging and supporting others in their times of bereavement. In the upheaval, there he was finding strength to turn around and give back showing others traversing the path of their own storms a guiding light.

Struggles can also unearth hidden talents, as in the case of Sarah, whose dyslexia had always made academic achievement an impossible task. Just as the caterpillar surrenders to the cocoon, she had to let go of her conventional approach to learning. In doing so, she found an affinity for coding, a language where she could excel. Today, she develops software that assists others with learning disabilities, showcasing not just her accomplishments, but her journey to self-acceptance and empowerment.

And then there is Marcus, a soldier who bore the physical as well as mental scars of war. Who went through the painful process of physical as well as mental rehab so much like that butterfly struggling out of its chrysalis. Now, he helps other veterans find their path to healing, using his adversity as a bridge to connect and uplift.

Amidst turmoil, there is Grace, whose family was torn by addiction. The chrysalis of her life seemed insurmountable, yet she emerged with a newfound purpose. Grace founded a community program that educates and supports families, turning her personal challenge into a community's beacon of hope.

Thomas faced a different kind of adversity. Misjudged and disregarded due to his background, he fought against a constant current of discrimination. Instead of succumbing, he became a lawyer, defending those who, like him, were unjustly treated. His adversities became his strengths, the very foundation of his unshakable resolve.

Rachel's story is one of her body's betrayals. A dancer, movement was her life's joy, snatched away by a sudden, debilitating illness. But Rachel's spirit danced on. She choreographed routines from her wheelchair, bringing inclusivity to the dance community and inspiring others to find harmony within their limitations.

For James, it was the invisible chains of debt that bound him. The pressure could have crushed him, but it instead ignited an entrepreneurial spark. He devised a financial planning tool that helps thousands manage their finances better. His financial burdens gave way to financial innovation.

Life handed Layla the challenge of single parenthood at a young age. The responsibility was like a cocoon, enveloping her in a myriad of obstacles. Through determination, she flourished, becoming a successful businesswoman and a role model for her child, redefining the narrative of young motherhood.

They are different stories, but all have a uniform thread—adversity was not the end but a beginning. Like of that chrysalis stage of a butterfly, it unravels untapped strength and beauty. And in yet, this transformation is not meant to be walked alone. There are communities, friends, and mentors, akin to the intricate network of nature that supports the butterfly's journey. Strength often comes from the collective, from shared experiences and mutual encouragement.

But the more we dig into these stories, it becomes apparent that the process of transformation is rarely a smooth or painless one. It asks of us everything we have and often things we never knew we possessed.

It is in this crucible of transformation that beauty is forged, and through it, a renewed capacity to soar is discovered.

It is not just 'survive' adversity; it is about 'thriving' despite how individuals transform their liabilities into assets, their losses into legacies, their pain into art. A profound alchemy, testimony of man's inventiveness and resilience and the indomitable will not to only go on but thrive.

In the pages that follow, these stories are not mere accounts but lights along the path. They serve as reminders that even in most challenging cocoon, we can find our wings, take flight, and emerge with a newfound grace. After all the beauty in adversity is not just what we endure but also of all we are during that process.

As we immerse ourselves further in these life-affirming narratives, we see a mosaic of the human experience. A vivid picture wherein every shade of challenge adds depth and contrast to the masterpiece that is life. They stand as beacons, illuminating the path forward for others who find themselves wrapped in the cocoon of hardship, guiding them toward their own incredible transformation.

The Concept of Post-Traumatic Growth and Resilience

Previously we discussed the different trials and tribulations of life with that akin to the stage of the cocoon as growth is not only imminent but necessarily crucial for some extraordinary to emerge. If the cocoon represents the struggle, then the concept of post-traumatic growth represents the magnificence that can be born from that struggle. Undoubtably so, it is in the fertile soil of our hardest experiences that seeds of resilience are planted and begin to take root.

Post traumatic growth as a counterintuitive phenomenon takes shape from distress. Just as strength enters the wings of the butterfly by the struggle required to emerge from its cocoon, many people often learn about their own hidden strength only after having faced adversity in life. Every struggle, every adversity carried within itself silent promise of new beginnings - isn't that a beauty of its own? Resilience, abundantly present in nature isn't just survival, but adapting, evolving, and flourishing. It's an individual's ability to stay against the gusts of change and proceed onward - inexplicably often - with a newer understanding and wider perception of what constitutes ones' identity and purpose.

This process, while painful, is not without purpose. In the churn and change, we are given the opportunity to reconstruct ourselves. Our values, beliefs, and philosophies can suddenly pivot, aligning more closely with the core truth of who we've discovered ourselves to be through the crucible of challenge.

Stories of post-traumatic growth are not mythical nor exceptional. They're scattered among us – in neighbors, friends, and even in the mirror. People who've faced loss, illness, or hardship, yet speak not just of survival but of a deeper sense of meaning that emerged from their trials reflect the very essence of this growth.

Recognizing that loss, and sorrow are interwoven threads in the fabric of life, gives a birth to resilience that propels post-traumatic growth, not being immune to pains. It's in the embracing, not the avoiding, of these elements that we begin to weave new patterns of understanding and emerge not despite the hardships but through them.

Yet, it's critical to acknowledge that growth after trauma is a deeply personal journey and that it doesn't come with a deadline. The chrysalis cannot be rushed, and the winged creature within must emerge in its own natural course. The metamorphosis is an individual rhythm much like the patterns and colors that adorn each butterfly's wings are unique to it alone.

Understanding post-traumatic growth is also understanding that we have reserves of strength previously untapped. There are levels of sympathy and compassion for both others and ourselves that emerge only when we've sailed through unnerving storms. Resilience is not an armor that guards us from damage, but rather a rich patina that forms over our previously untested metal, showing that it has been tempered by fire and thus holds a new form.

In this context, resilience is not a static quality but an active endeavor. Even as forces pitch those tipping stones up and send us flying off course, by the moment but we are always moving back toward wherever it is we are trying to go. Our hard-won resilience is the compass that guides us back, time and again, to our path.

And let's not forget – resilience is not solely the product of an individual spirit. It's often kindled and nurtured by those around us, a reflection of the interconnectedness experienced within a community or support system. A single butterfly flutters amidst many, all part of a greater migration, each supporting the other in subtle, yet profound ways.

Enveloped in the folds of adversity, we are not alone. Shared stories of resilience and growth remind us that in our struggles, we are united. We find comfort in the shared human experience – knowing that others too have walked through the fire and have come out not only intact but transformed.

In acceptance of post-traumatic growth, we start seeing not only the beauty but potential of those scars. We start appreciating the unfound joys and strengths that have blossomed out from our adversities. The ability to survive storms is not the main thing; it's more about thriving when the clouds have parted, and the sun shines once again upon us.

Trauma changes us, and yet, we navigate these changes as the butterfly trusts its instinct to fly; gracefully embracing its journey, resilient to the vagaries of the wind. This is the ultimate act of hope and trust - believing in whatever there lies on the other side of sorrow and pain so powerful beauty. As our story bridges into the next chapter of resilience, let us carry with us the profound understanding that, though the night may be long, the dawn is inevitable. It's the perpetual cycle of life, mirrored in the delicate yet determined flight of butterflies – the journey of growth through resilience.

So next in the story, let us take a closer examination of the wings of resilience; those delicate but yet strong appendages that permit the butterfly - and oh so often, the human spirit - to ascend to a place wherefrom to rise above the landscapes that once had him pinned down beneath its cruelty. Therein lies the potential for both flight and transcendent beauty.

Ways in Which Obstacles becomes Catalysts for Personal Development

The stories serve as a reference point for this section, which explores the ways people grow through suffering. This article's job is to study how problems might help make us more aware of ourselves, harder against tough times and grow stronger from inside. Readers can learn more about their own growth and how hard times help them, by seeing connections between the troubles people go through to life changes a butterfly makes before it becomes an adult.

Like how a butterfly changes, the troubles we face in life can help us grow on our own. Like a bug changes many times before looking exactly like a beautiful butterfly, our problems and struggles can help us know ourselves better. They also contribute to changing who we are for the good.

1. Self-reflection: When we meet problems, our thoughts, feelings and actions remind us to think about them. We start to wonder about our decisions, thoughts and what we value. We try to find out more about who are deep down inside of us. By thinking deeply about us, we can find parts to get better or grow. This helps us understand more about who we are.

2. Identifying strengths and weaknesses: Usually, we have to leave our safe places when problems come up. This makes us face the things that are hard for us. From these happenings, we learn about our good points and bad points. We find out about skills we didn't know before, strength in handling tough times and things inside us. These might be new to discover. At the same time, we understand are there things that need to change and improve. This helps us know what areas should be worked on for our own growth.

3. Cultivating empathy and compassion: Fights in our own lives can cause us to understand better and feel more for others dealing with the same problems. While dealing with our own challenges, we become more aware of the problems faced by people nearby. This increased feeling for others helps to create a sense of caring and wishing to help and lift up friends. This helps us grow as a person, because it deepens our connection with other people and opens up more ways to look at life.

4. Prioritizing personal values: Problems can make us break from our normal ways and force us to think again about what's important in life. We start to ask ourselves what's really important in our lives and how we should put things first. This reflection on self helps us find our true values again and make sure we are acting with sincere feelings. By concentrating on

what's really important, we can choose actions that help us grow as people and guide us to a more joyful life.

5. Building resilience and adaptability: Like how a butterfly comes out from its shell, our struggles can make us stronger and more able to change. Every difficulty we get past make us better at dealing with coming challenges. We learn to like change, get better at solving problems and build a way of thinking that sees challenges as chances for getting bigger. This makes us stronger people, helping us grow by giving us more self-confidence and the ability to face problems.

Life's problems can be like a change that turns us into something new. Just like how caterpillars turn into butterflies. By thinking about ourselves, finding what we do best and worst, feeling how others feel with care and kindness, choosing what is most important to us personally in our lives at least shows how we are developing as people. We grow by understanding who we are. This journey leads those willing well-rendered deeds like good moral success within their own heart work combined continue moving ahead into a more fortunate life. Including as we go through life's problems; we start to know more about ourselves and see how these events help for growth.

This chapter looked at how the problems we have, and the butterfly's change are similar. Like a cat-eye goes through many steps to change into a lovely butterfly, we all have our own process when taking on problems. We learn more about ourselves and what we can do when we struggle with hard things. This helps us know where we fit in the world better.

When we think about our feelings and moves, it helps us to learn more about what makes them strong or weak. We find out things about ourselves that we probably didn't know before. This helps us grow as people. Our own troubles help us learn to feel for others. This makes it easier to understand people and have important friendships, which helps us grow as a person figuring out what matters most to us and making sure we behave true to who we are can help make our lives more meaningful. When we think again about what is important to us, we make decisions on purpose. These help us grow as people and bring us nearer to the things that matter most including goals and dreams in our life. These choices help make us feel more satisfied and successful.

Maybe most important, the problems we handle make us strong and flexible inside. Each issue we beat helps us get stronger and brighter. This makes it easier to fight future problems with courage and stubbornness. We learn to accept change and see problems as chances for improvement instead of something that stops us. This toughness helps us grow in our lives and gives us the power to face life's changing world with dignity.

Final thoughts, the struggles we face in our lives can change us in amazing ways. Just like a butterfly changes, our troubles help us know ourselves better. They make others feel what we do and they show what is most important to each of for all stays strong no matter how hard life gets. . . . It's bit Fancy). Taking the word and using changes lets us learn more, withstand problems better. It makes us focused on affecting growth of heart-centered ideas while standing tougher from obstacles open our hearts wider in thinking just like those few important days in life that teach great knowledge when we get over difficult issues for them easier than ahead times before a due date when finding comforts among things understood Like the butterfly coming out of its shell, we can also come out stronger from our problems and ready to experience growth in humans.

This chapter was intended to make people see that there is good in life's struggles or mistakes or when things go wrong. It doesn't make them feel like a problem, but as ways to change lives for the better. People are told to speak about their own problems with more care for the strength that comes from being open and change happening in difficult times of life.

Chapter 4:
Resilience Wings

In the grand theater of existence, where challenges dance with fortitude, the butterfly emerges as a masterful performer, unfazed by the trials that precede its flight. Just as the creature must summon an innate resilience to thrust forth from its chrysalis, we too must harness this vigilant spirit within our own lives. This chapter will not venture into the maze of what resilience *is*—for that narrative has been woven prior—but rather, it will take flight into the realm of **how** resilience operates, functioning much like the delicate yet robust wings of our winged mentor. We'll delve into the marrow of our trials, exploring the silent strength that carries us aloft when the winds of hardship seek to cast us down. The butterfly teaches that it's not about avoiding the storm, but finding the courage to spread our wings *within* it, understanding that the fibers of our wings are forged stronger in the tempest. As we journey through this chapter, let the mystique of the butterfly's effortless glide inspire our own path toward unyielding resilience, reminding us that it's with weathered wings we soar highest and with grace we discover the potential nestled within our own life's cocoon.

Resilience as a Key to Transformation

Art of change, · the butterfly emerging form its chrysalis, is a subtle grace that speaks to the core what it means to be resilience. Resilience, the very fabric of which our wings of transformation are woven, serves not as a mere catalyst for change but as the foundation for profound growth and metamorphosis. It is through resilience that we, too, can unfurl our wings and ascend to new heights of personal realization.

Picture the butterfly, exemplar of resilience, which endures the confines of a cocoon in its larval stage, only to be reborn with wings brilliant and robust. This resilience, inherent to us all, is a potent force, able to shepherd us through the tumult of our cocoons, the challenges, struggles, and times of uncertainty that inevitably come to define segments of our lives.

Really, the proof of resilience is acknowledging persistence in the face of adversity. The transformation pathway does not offer a linear and simple ease to travel upon. There would be found countless impeding blocks and trying circumstances that would test our built-on strength and commitment. Nevertheless, a choice sits waiting in these very trials to emerge as profound transformation out of the cocoon of our personal struggles. Where the butterfly must have some great strength to muster for such a graceful creature simply to breaking free of its silken prison, so too should we. These moments of pressure and constriction do not aim to crush us but instead forge us into stronger, more complete versions of ourselves. Each adversity faced with grace and resolve contributes another layer to the fortitude of our wings.

This fortitude, a testament to our resilience, is not innately gifted in generous supply, but rather cultivated through each small act of bravery. Whether that bravery is waking up each morning when engulfed in sorrow or the arduous climb out of financial ruin, every chapter of our journey that necessitates resilience is an opportunity for growth.

Besides, our resilience begets an internal transformation which is often imperceptible at first. A similar way to the metamorphosis of a butterfly underneath the opaque chrysalis so are our own changes. Yet, with time, they burgeon forth, materializing in newfound wisdom, strength, and a beauty that is uniquely our own.

Weaving resilience into the fabric of our being allows us to adapt to our circumstances just as butterflies have adapted to the world around them over millennia. With each generational flutter, they have encountered vast climates and terrains, forging ahead with an inbuilt resilience that rivals any creature on earth.

Our inspiration should be to be like the butterfly of adaptability, to remain flexible in our thinking, to throw out old notions that no longer serve us and to stay open to spiritedly run into the evolution of our convictions that leads us toward our dreams. The purpose is beckoning to be reborn in the face of change, grow and learn, and reach beyond, more than ever before.

Maybe, as well resilience is about recover, it's the ability to bounce back in life's umpteenth tests stronger and a little wiser, bit more patient and profoundly more empathetic. The essence of true transformation lies within our ability to recover, mend wings, and use scars as lessons not limitations.

Because through this experience of life we are reminded that resilience is not a human resource that one person has in limited quantity. It gets fed anew with every challenge confronted, every dispiriting obstacle overcome. The supply of these rejuvenating cycles in life is without end and therefore offers us infinite opportunities to be reformed, transformed.

For the very same reason many butterflies have indeed come to symbolize hope across religions and civilizations, our personal stories of tenacity have often become beacons other people follow. Sharing the struggles that we have come over and the strength we got may shed light on some people's journey which they may be going through a hard time.

In our moments of greatest strain, it's crucial to remind ourselves that every struggle brings with it the seeds of growth. These seeds need but resilience to germinate, and, in time, they will blossom into experiences and qualities that allow us to rise above our former selves.

Also, and the process of transformation through resilience is never to be rushed. Just in the same way, don't help the butterfly out of the cocoon, let's also honor the natural progression of our personal growth. Impatience can lead to premature, brittle wings that lack the strength to soar. Our journey must unfold in its due time, revealing its beauty in the moments when we are ready to embrace it fully.

If we are resilient, sky is just the limit as to how possibilities will be there for our transformation. May we not strive just to withstand the storm but thrive within it - tapping an inner strength we never knew existed. Not just the journey to transformation but resilient is the greatest transformation of all. If we may keep emerging let us never forget our very wings were made from resilient.

Learning from the Butterfly's Ability to Adapt

In the preceding chapters, we explored the profound transformation that lies within the cocoon of challenges and the unparalleled change signified by metamorphosis. As we continue our journey, we encounter another crucial aspect of the butterfly's existence: its incredible ability to adapt. Observing this small creature's adaptability offers a glimpse into the resilient nature that is also within us.

From crawling as a caterpillar, the butterfly begins life grounded, eventually gaining wings to propel it through the air. This is less a literal change of form than an entirely new definition of possibilities - it teaches embracing differences and striving not simply to survive, but to flourish within them.

So, adaptation is not a passive process but feelings which the individual engages with features of the surroundings wherein it lives. The butterfly, for example, is free from any regret towards its crawling life when it was a caterpillar. The other examples include its development period inside the cocoon. Instead, it spreads the wings and learnt the currents of the air and embraces every breeze as a guidepost to new destinations.

Seasons change, flowers come and go but the butterfly adapts its flight, its feeding pattern, even its mating behavior. There therein lies a great lesson: adaptation requires an acute sense of one's environment. Just as it is important to mimic the adaptability that the butterfly shows in the face of changed conditions, humans too must engender an awareness that perceives change as part and parcel of the very fabric of life.

Just as the butterfly encounters varied climates and terrains, people experience the vagaries of life. Some events are as balmy as spring; others carry the chill of anomaly or loss. In these moments, the very essence of adaptability isn't just to endure but to find ways to navigate and flourish.

Furthermore, the butterfly does not adapt out of fear but rather from a place of intrinsic strength. This strength is the resilience we so admire—the capability to transform challenge into opportunity. Through each wind, through each downpour, resilience becomes the steady beat of its wings.

When life ushers in the unexpected and unfamiliar, the normal response can be one of resistance. Yet, consider the butterfly: it does not resist the wind; it harnesses it. Adopting this mindset can shift our perspective, turning obstacles into winds that elevate us to new heights.

Resilience is not an in build or a genetic trait but a cultivation, accumulation or result of so many minute victories against the storms that hit life. Every struggle that does not take the spirit from us, every dark moment that we transcend is equivalent to wing strengthening before a flight.

Just as the butterfly must rest to let its wings dry and strengthen before it is able to take off, so moments of our own reflective rest are equally crucial. But doubt and uncertainty are only natural, yet we might also arise from the dew of contemplation with no small sense of purpose and direction.

At times, the butterfly's environment may change so drastically that old behaviors no longer serve. Change is inescapable, but adaptation is a choice. It is in choosing to adapt that we exercise our freedom—a freedom to evolve, to reimagine our lives in the face of change.

Consider the migratory paths of certain butterfly species, a phenomenon that reveals adaptability on an astonishing scale. Despite countless generations, each butterfly instinctively knows its course. Here we uncover another fact about adaptability: it is sometimes wired into the essence of beings. Similarly, within each of us lies a navigational instinct that, if heeded, can guide us through life's labyrinth.

Adaptation also involves shedding the unnecessary—the way a butterfly leaves behind its chrysalis. As it takes to the air, it does not encumber itself with past layers. Thus, to truly adapt, we must discern what needs to be let go so we may ascend unburdened towards our aspirations.

It is not that the beauty of the butterfly is dimmed by its adaption but made more beautiful in this dance with these elements. In a very similar way, when we adapt with grace, we cease to just survive - we infuse our lives and our existence with a unique beauty formed beneath the pressures and the molds of life experience.

Let the butterfly's resilience inspire your own wings. Adaptation does not imply losing oneself; it signifies an evolution of identity with each challenge faced, each transition navigated, each new dawn greeted with eyes wide open and wings ready to unfurl.

In integrating the butterfly's adaptability into our lives, we do not merely cope with change—we celebrate it. We evolve with it. And we fly—sometimes tentatively at first, only to find ourselves soaring with newfound strength, resilience, and a profound appreciation for the journey.

Cultivating Resilience in the Face of Hardship

Amidst the battles that life presents, the essence of resilience emerges like newfound wings, sculpted by the trials of the cocoon, defined by adversity. While we go through our own cycles of growth and hardship, instances will stare at us in the face that brought to the fore nothing short of the deep well of inner strength in us. the tempests that weather our core. Resilience, much like the delicate yet determined butterfly, is cultivated over time through persistence and the unwavering belief in the possibility of flight, despite the tempests that weather our being.

Hardship shapes us in ways we often can't predict. It sculpts our character, as the chisel of time hones a sculpture into form. In its grasp, we can find ourselves feeling as fragile as a butterfly's wing, yet it is precisely in these moments that we discover an innate power. As the butterfly does not shy from the rain, neither should we falter at the touch of sorrow. Instead, we learn to dance in the storm's embrace, understanding that without it, the path to resilience remains untrodden.

The periled way of the caterpillar inexorably inched toward that transformative reprieve of chrysalis. Humans too, are called to embrace the encasings wrecked from our challenges. From inside out, turns the caterpillar turning in seclusion, building the inner strength: bravery to transform. Like-wise, have to search ourself for that courage to weather and ultimately overpower the bitter storm of adversities.

Our narratives may differ, but the threads of struggle weave through each like a tapestry of unified experience. One might tell of loss and the subsequent rediscovery of self, while another speaks of failure birthing steely determination. These stories are vital, for it is through the shared odyssey of the human spirit that we may each find solace and inspiration to cultivate our resilience.

To engender this resilience, one must first acknowledge the role of pain. We must not shun our bruises but rather peer into them with a kind of sacred curiosity. For it is through understanding the impact of our wounds that we can begin to heal and fortify ourselves against the inequities of our journeys.

In the realm of perseverance, patience stands as a silent sentinel. Just as the butterfly bodes its time until – with wings largely incomplete within the confines of the chrysalis – it is ready to unfurl forth on the blossoming natural spring landscape, so too do we need to practice patience with ourselves and also in the circumstances that envelop us. The timing of our emergence into strength cannot be rushed; it must unfold in its divine temporality.

Developing hope is one of the major key majors to the nurturing of resilience. It's that flicking flame that defiantly dances in the face of the howling wind. Hope anchors us, audacity gives brave us the hope to dream of a sunrise in the bleakest of nights and persistence the audacity to go forward towards it.

And the community, too, is a crucible for resilience. So that the interconnection of life, itself, is a testimony that we are not alone in our plight. Like the ecosystem, perhaps, we may liken ourselves to an intricate network as well that will grow and flourish, mutually needing and providing nurture – the butterfly can only really survive not in seclusion but amidst the vital complexity of life.

If the butterfly has to apply this kind of effort in process of breaking free from its chrysalis, then we too have to apply will power to come out of adversity. It's not a joke and a piece of cake by any means, without struggle but still breaking free is an undisputed witness of resilience. Our will is our wings, through which we liberate ourselves from the confines of our challenges.

The ability to change and adapt is a sign of strength and the fine skill of being flexible without snapping. As the seasons change, butterflies adapt their behavior to take advantage of rather than fight against nature. Along with everyone else, we must learn to adapt, to set and modify our sails when life throws us a curveball.

Self-compassion is an essential factor to consider when facing adversity. It should be noted that it is always nice to treat ourselves well since we are usually our own worst enemies. The soft touch of self-compassion nurtures the growth of sturdy resilience wings.

Thus, such mindfulness and reflection are akin to nurturing sunshine and rain that allows the natural beings to grow and blossom. In other words, as we move our attention toward the present through reflecting on our experiences, it is like adding water that exactly nourishes these seeds of resilience in the hopes that maybe they can grow in even the most driftwood or barren environment.

Hardship has the potential to diminish or to distinguish. The choice lies within our hands—or rather, our minds. The paths we tread are often unexpected, but our reaction to adversity can transform obstacles into the very stepping stones of our resilience.

Boundaries, both physical and emotional, must sometimes be established to preserve and foster resilience. Much like a butterfly guards against the elements, we must protect our inner garden, ensuring that while open to the world, we are not left defenseless against it.

Growing resilient is to see the wisdom in the journey itself. Every struggle, every heartache holds within it the seeds of enlightenment themselves in whose planting bring forth the fruit of deep personal development. As the butterfly teaches us, the real beauty of resilience is not for the endurance but in the deep transformative it may cause. With wings emboldened by conquered, trial soars into the skies of our lives as testimonial beings of thence power and grace with which resilience endows in face of hardship.

Chapter 5:
Unfurling Wings of Resilience

In the tender light of dawn, the once confined caterpillar emerges, adorned in a miraculous set of wings—resilience incarnate. The struggle within the chrysalis, an intense transformation often mistaken for the end, is but the birth of magnificence. And so as we begin to emerge and unfurl the wings of our own resilience, let us delve into the sophisticated framework of strength and flexibility which composes a butterfly's wings. It's a fabric woven by adversity, each thread a testament to survival and the ability to rebound from the pressures of the cocoon. Our life's setbacks, much like the cellular changes within the chrysalis, are not merely obstacles, but catalysts for growth. In this chapter, we're not just observers of the butterfly's metamorphosis; we're invited to spread our own wings. To breathe deeply the air of challenge, and adopt the fortitude of these winged wonders, as we prepare to soar into our own boundless skies.

Using the Butterfly's Wings as a Metaphor for Developing Resilience

Reflect upon the creature of butterfly, an ethereal creature its wings delicate and bright carry's it from flower to flower in a delicate hop of survival. These wings though seemingly fragile, are robust structures that confer upon the butterfly its renowned resilience in the face of its environment's ever-shifting caprices. Similarly, it's worth exploring how, like the wings of a butterfly, the human spirit can develop resilience, a strength that makes the daunting winds of adversity navigable.

Miraculously though, a caterpillar can undergo a significant change into a butterfly just like that. To come through this type of ordeal with no marks or scars to your conscience one needs all the inner strength you can muster. It is therefore a journey fraught with vulnerability and the necessity of an inner strength to emerge successfully on the other side. The wings must be strong enough to bear the body into its new realm; so too must individuals cultivate a resilience capable of sustaining them through the unknown realms of their personal experiences.

The butterfly's wings are damp and wrinkled at the time of emergence from its cocoon because of its existence in the larval stage before the impending change. The insect must instantly pump life into its wings to meet the acute need to strengthen them. This act is critical for survival; much akin to how humans must foster their inner resources when facing the soggy, wrinkled challenges life presents. Resilience involves expanding one's capabilities, pushing the lifeblood of hope and perseverance into areas weakened by trials.

It's crucial to acknowledge that a butterfly's wings, while delicate, are resilient by design. Their structure is made up of many overlapping layers and scales that contribute to their strength and aerodynamics. The complicated humans we are today are the result of the various good and terrible events that both good and bad people have had throughout their lives. Personal determination and or the essence of being resilient, like the shimmering of butterfly wings, is a beautiful thing, especially when it shows how a person's character shines through after they've overcome adversity.

Additionally, butterflies must practice using their wings in preparation for flight. They don't simply sprout wings and soar; there's a learning curve that requires patience and effort. It's not something that you are born to have or lack it without being present but being resilient is a skill that can be build up with time and effort had put into it.

It is not unlikely to conclude turbulence is a common experience in our world, but what counts most is how we deal with it like the butterflies do. Like the butterfly, we must learn to adjust our flight patterns, to use the resistance to climb higher rather than be defeated by it. A life devoid of challenges would yield neither the strength nor grace of a butterfly's flight—the same challenges we face can lead us to discover our own strength and grace.

Butterflies do not resist the wind but allow it to lift them to greater heights; adaptation is essential. A very important lesson, which needs to be learnt in developing resilience is that we need to adapt to every twist and turn of the life's flow, its ups and downs. Just as the butterfly is dependent on the wind currents to transport, similarly do require faith in our own capabilities of surfing through the waves of life.

Another key aspect is that a butterfly's wings can regenerate if damaged; this natural repair process shows that resilience is not about never being hurt but about the capacity to heal and carry on. Healing, then, becomes an active component of resilience—it's about mending the tears in our wings and lifting off once again, perhaps more cautious but also wiser and stronger.

While resting, butterflies often close their wings to protect the more delicate underside. What is helpful about this intentional unwinding and protective approach is it demonstrates that self-care isn't indulgent, but what's necessary. Building resilience really means, after all, taking the time to charge up and rethink and gear up for coming challenges.

In their migratory journeys, butterflies cover vast distances, guided by internal instinct. This endurance is inspirational, indicating that resilience includes the will to continue despite the fatigue and the myriad of obstacles that may lie ahead. It's a process of trusting the internal compass that guides one through life's migrations and transformations.

Just as a butterfly must contend with predators and other threats, individuals face the perils of their environments—societal pressures, personal losses, and internal battles. Resilience provides the means not only to survive these threats but to emerge transformed, much like a butterfly, ready to inspire with the beauty of its wings and the power of its flight.

Moreover, no two butterflies have the same pattern of wing, so it is in understanding that no two people's journey to resilience will be the same. Although some patterns may be loud and glaring many of them can also be quite unassuming and delicate. Being resilient, it is not one-size-fits-all, but rather a very individual path that exists in very individual ways for people.

The butterfly also possesses tenacity and while the pollen left off it, as from visiting the flowers, the pollen helps them thrive, at the same time it improves its environment. The courage, tenacity, and composure under fire of a particular individual can inspire others to be the same, which will possibly benefit the entire community.

As with the lifecycle of the butterfly, resilience is not a destination but a continuous evolution. We are perpetually in a state of becoming, of stretching our wings toward the sunlight and rising on the thermals of our challenges. With every flutter, we are rewriting our narratives, embracing a state of constant change and growth—a testament to the power of our inner strength and adaptability.

Hence, the butterfly, with its potent symbolism and the silent strength of its wings, stands as a testament to the potential within each of us. A potential that transforms, adapts, endures, and ultimately, takes flight into a life marked by robust, unfailing resilience. An Potential that mutates, evolves, endures, and finally surges into a life strengthened by unwavering resilience. It should be in our bearing to be as graceful like a butterfly and be purposive as we gravitate towards the future on wings that we have forged from the womb of adversities, ready to take flight into the limitless sky.

Exploring the Role of Resilience in Overcoming Setbacks and Achieving Personal Goals

As a butterfly goes through its life cycle, similarly our very existence is a sequence of trials and tribulations that only makes us stronger with a greater sense of perseverance. As we delve into these events, we cannot fail to notice that resilience is not all about getting up back on feet, it's about moving forward, turning failures into victories and reaching our lofty personal goals.

Think of a butterfly fighting tooth and nail to come out of its cocoon - powerful metaphor for unsquash able human spirit ever thirsty of success against all odds. Through unexpected situations, we draw strength to persevere and find out inner resources that we did not know existed; that is the power of resilience.

But what propels us to rise after a fall? What makes us choose suffering in order to become stronger in the long run? This story explores these questions, unveiling the sophisticated arras of human resiliency that allows us not only to survive but to also thrive in many brutal realities of life.

The power of resilience is multi-faceted—it's found in the quiet introspection following a loss, in the passionate pursuit of goals despite repeated failures, and in the gentle acceptance of change that we didn't ask for. In every setback, there are seeds of regrowth, silently waiting to sprout into a garden of opportunities.

To build resilience is to learn the art of patience. Much like the patiently metamorphosing creature, it requires a gentle acknowledgment that progress is a slow incubation, not an over-night transformation. It entails recognizing that each step back can become a setup for a grander leap forward if navigated with wisdom and courage.

Resilience is also closely woven to the web of our relationships with support systems. Just like a butterfly dines on nectar from flowers in order to sustain it, we derive strength that comes along with encouragement and love surrounding us. Our connections will buoy our spirits and provide refuge when our own wings feel too fragile to bear the brunt of turbulence in life.

Developing resilience often requires the essence of a deep dive into self-awareness, where one confronts their flaws and fears. It is within that particularly intimate exploration we begin to reshape our narratives learning every scar may be a testament of survival and every tear can irrigate the soil where a new dream germinates.

When obstacles look too difficult to face and our dreams seem distant from our realities, It is the spirit of perseverance that says" One more try." It's the intuitive knowing that the hardest climbs lead to most rewarding scenic vistas, and that the path to success is string with tenacity.

At times, resilience manifests as a quiet revolution against the cynicism that the world often espouses. In the face of dismissive voices, choosing to persist with optimism is nothing short of radical defiance—a refusal to be cocooned in a narrative of defeat.

Indeed, because resilience is a process of facing pain and emerging from it better off than before, to cultivate it does not mean to false-face away the fact or somehow plead it out of existence. It means looking at the hurt in light of the world, cradling it gently, yet refusing to allow it to man the helm. This delicate balance is what can steer us towards the calm waters of healing and growth.

Goals, personal and professional and spiritual -- derivations of striving, they are touchstones on our journey towards fulfillment. They act like compass points guiding us through the wilderness of life's trials. Resilience is the unwavering determination which drives to push against all odds in our search of how to live righteously according to the dictates of conscience and heart.

In this culture that idolizes the final product, resilience calls upon our value of journey over destination. Our focus is removed from the lone high point to the patchwork of intermediate successes and lessons learned. that make-up the journey to our goals.

The lack of vulnerability is not necessarily a sign of resilience; let us not be fooled. On the contrary, it's accepting that weakness of ours and know that even when we're spent, inside of us beats a force stronger than the one trying to put us down which can help us fly above the storm beat after beat.

Building resilience is a deeply personal quest, an internal dialogue that resonates with the eternal dance between strength and vulnerability. This inner journey is very much similar to a great transformation of a butterfly - it changes us from the inside and as we come out of our struggle 'cocoon', become stronger and mature.

Lastly, in times when we all face some challenges in life let's just remember that every act of resilience takes us closer to ultimate dreams which we aspire for. Taking advantage of the attitude itself is a first step in opening our wings and reach for a growing limitless potential.

Offering Strategies for Building and Strengthening One's Resilience

As one looks closer at the inspection of the tender essence of our unfurling resilience, we find that cultivating such strength is much like the steady, patient revitalization of a garden. It is an intentional act, a gentle nurturing of the attributes within us that can outlast the ravages of life. Resilience, very much like those delicate patterns on a butterfly's wing, needs to be cultivated with intent, grace, and determination. But lying at the heart of resilience is this basic truth— that our reactions shape our paths far more than any adverse situation does.

To instill resilience, we begin with reflection; we look inward and ask ourselves how we have handled strife in days past. In these quiet moments of contemplation, recognize that every challenge is an invitation to rise, much like the butterfly heeds the call of the vast skies.

We need to acknowledge our emotions in the face of hardship - to let oneself feel fear, sadness, anger – yet not to let them define or confine us. Emotional resilience is a dance of vulnerability; it is about being authentic in our experiences yet not allowing emotions to wield undue influence over our actions.

Communication too is a centerpiece in this process. Seek the solace found in shared stories and listen to the thrum of human experience. Speak your truth, for every word uttered is a step toward understanding and a chisel sculpting your inner fortitude. Engage in this exchange as if the world itself converses with you through the whisperings of friends, the guidance of mentors, and the silence between words of solace.

We should never underrate the influence of mind, developing an optimistic view is to efforts and perseverance like sunshine is to be hatching of a butterfly. Foster an internal dialogue of encouragement and affirmation. When the mind weaves tales of doubt and fear, reshape these narratives with a poise borne of self-assured strength.

Moreover, resilience can be fortified through action. Define your boundaries, identify your core values, and live in accordance to these guiding principles. It is in the calm assertion of one's beliefs that a robust resilience is born, like the fresh bloom which stands resolute amongst the wilds.

Adaptability, it can be a quality of the resilient being, it's not breaking down under the weight of change but graciously managing your way through the unpredictable. Set up your sails and change course once the wind changes, same as a butterfly with his fragile wings which allow him to shift a direction.

Knowledge, too, is a bastion of resilience. Arm yourself with information about the situations and stressors you face. Understanding equips you with foresight, and with foresight, you can preempt the waves of distress before they become tempests.

Do not underestimate the importance of nurturing your physical vessel. Care for your body through nourishment, rest, and exercise; it is the sanctuary wherein your spirit resides, and only a temple properly tended can sustain its divinity.

In this odyssey of resilience, others play a pivotal role. Cultivate a support network of kindred souls, of hearts forged in compassion and understanding. Just like being in the flowers' symbiotic relationships allows the butterfly to flourish, so do we flourish supported by community tethered together by mutual respect and love.

Integration of a spiritual or meditative practice can also serve as a bastion against life's upheavals. Whether through prayer, mindfulness, or simply quiet contemplation, these moments of reprieve grant us clarity and solace, and in solace is found the might to persist.

And let us not forget about the arts—music, literature, painting—all profound channels for expression and healing. Engage with creativity as if it were a second language; let it speak to you, for you, and about you.

Above everything, resilience does not mean to do away with the distress but into the capability to move on even when the distress is present. It is the acknowledgment that suffering has and will always be a permanent thread in human existence. Yet within that acknowledgement is found the strength to weave a narrative of courage and hope.

Practice resilience as with the same reverence a painter applies on his canvas; every stroke, a lesson learned, every hue an emotion weathered. With each paintbrush of resilience, the canvas of your life strokes into a masterpiece of human spirit as grand and breathtaking, with wingspan in mid-flutter like that of the butterfly against azure skies.

Resilience, then, is not just a trait but a living, breathing process—it is the continual return to the skies, no matter how powerful the storm. It is the silent resolve that after the tempest, one will emerge, not unscarred or unscathed, but undeniably stronger, with wings wide, ready once again to ascend.

Chapter 6:
Soaring Beyond Limitations

Having unfurled the resilient wings of past struggles, we now ascend to the realm of 'Soaring Beyond Limitations', where we shed the chrysalis of constraint to reveal an expanse of potential. Here we are not bound by the gravity of self-doubt or the whispers of the incredulous wind. This chapter is an anthem of emancipation, an invitation to quell the dissonant voices that have long kept us ground-bound. Truly, such is the idea that has been discussed so far, that the space between the present and the future can be as narrow as a butterfly's wing. Just as our flying natural contemporaries have shown us through their existence, restrictions are but surreal walls that one can pass through without too much of a hassle if there really is faith and resolve. As we glide through these pages, let the tender currents of these words guide you through self-discovery to that liberating vista where boundless skies wait patiently. It is there, in that sacred space of freedom, that the contours of your dreams carve their silhouettes against the horizon and your spirit can dance upon the air, unrestrained and utterly infinite.

Unleashing Personal Potential

The ascension from elongated pauses in our lives, where moments stretch on as though they were themselves the chrysalis of time, leads us into the realm of personal potential. Potential is the whispered promise of the caterpillar before it submits itself to the silence of transformation. Across the textures of our lived experiences, we reach a pivotal intersection where we choose to unfurl the tenacity of our spirit.

True potential, much like the butterfly's instinctual urge to break free, is often encased within self-imposed boundaries, formidable yet fragile. The awakening of the force inside of us is a delicate maneuver, a gentle coaxing of the soul, asking it to rise, to shake off the dust not so much of our natural weaknesses but of our doubts and limitations. The crux of what we can become perches eagerly upon the decisions we make in the solitude of our cocoons.

But to rise above the ordinary and become great requires extraordinary faith in one's self. You become your own architect constructing the scaffolding that will support your ascendancy. This power to believe, this trust in her burgeoning wings is not bred from the mirrored reflections of the world but carried by the quiet truths that sing in the heart during the darkest hours of introspection.

As we unveil our personal capacities, we embrace the paradox of strength found in vulnerability. There is an ethereal quality in admitting to oneself the extent and capacity of one's power. Within this acknowledgment rests the energy that propels one forward, out into the clearing, under the wide expanse of possibility.

Yet how does one marshal this energy? It starts with the cultivation of self-awareness, the garden from which clarity blossoms. Knowing one's own capabilities, eccentricities, temperament and reactions to the ever changing world around them is the essence of being self-aware.

You must not shy away from the reflection presented by failure and the depth it adds to your understanding. Each misstep is a conversation with destiny, a lesson dressed in the cloak of experience. Let it teach you. Let it shape the sinews of your determination.

Language, spoken to the self, plays a pivotal role. Your words wield the power to construct realities. Infuse your internal dialogue with confidence and conviction, choose phrases that uplift rather than undermine. The narrative you endorse is the life you live out.

And so, you are called to set goals that reach past the tepid waters of the easy, swimming into the currents of what challenges you, what refines you. Goals are not mere endpoints but are illuminations on a path that leads ever upwards, each achieved goal a lamppost glowing with satisfaction and beckoning toward the next.

Belonging to a community where dreams are shared, and encouragement flows freely, can amplify your journey. Align yourself with those who strive with a similar intensity and purpose, those who challenge you and applaud your progress. The collective vibe of aspiration is a powerful catalyst for growth.

Preparing for the unpredictable, the inevitable winds of change and adversity, is another indispensable part of releasing your potential. Adaptability is not the abandonment of your core, but rather the flexible dance of your spirit with the unknown a learned rhythm, a harmony with the shifting tides.

However, gratitude, in small, understated ways otherwise overlooked, plays a pivotal role in bringing out the full potential within. Thankfulness can change perspective; what was once now an obstacle becomes opportunity. Appreciate the now for duty's inherent potential; gratitude anchors one to the workshop of the present, the only workshop where all potentials can be wrought.

It is crucial to recognize that unleashing potential does not occur in the monochrome tones of isolation. Perspective is gained through the kaleidoscopic views offered by varied experiences and relationships. Potential is not a solitary flame; it is a fire fed by a rich assortment of insights and interactions.

The timing of your pursuits, as with the emergence of a butterfly, is delicate. There is a dance to be performed with patience, knowing

U. E. David MBA, MDiv.

when to surge forward and when to yield to the rhythm of preparation. Honor your pace—some wings take longer to dry in the sun but how resplendently they shine once aloft!

Finally, as you stand at the precipice of what you can be, remember the journey. Remember the struggle that gave rise to the very wings you now possess. Your potential is a mosaic of every trial and triumph. With your inner compass set, you have the latitude to navigate your purpose, erecting a life that reaches for the expanse of blue that invites you to claim your place within it.

Unleashing your personal potential, therefore, is honesty in action. It is the sincere and relentless pursuit of 'becoming' threaded through every fiber of your being. It is vitality. It is the courage found in the silence of one's soul, where the truest versions of ourselves reside, waiting to spread their wings under the affirming skies of our choices.

Breaking Free from Self-imposed Constraints

At some point in life, we will all reach to a phase of our life where the things that were hindrances to us at some points are no more capable of defining us just like the final phases of a butterfly's transformation. The cocoon, a safe haven of development and self-reflection, eventually becomes a restraint. It is then we realize the essential act of breaking free—yet, it is often not the cocoon imposed by nature we struggle against, but one of our own making.

This self-constructed cocoon is woven from threads of doubt, fear, and self-criticism. It is a protective shell anchored in our psyche, created to safeguard us from potential failure and hurt. One might ponder on the deep irony there—it is the very safeguard meant to protect us that ends up being the barrier keeping us from soaring to new heights. Indeed, the constraints we impose on ourselves can be harder to transcend than any external limits.

The call to break free is an awakening to the realization that we are our chief saboteurs. It is acknowledging the whisper of will that says, 'We are more than this.' The recognition that the only approval truly necessary is from within starts a revolution in the soul, where old beliefs and fears are overthrown, and the heart is reinstated as the rightful ruler of one's aspirations.

Peering into the heart's deepest desires requires a candidness that might leave us feeling exposed. However, through this lens that does not waver from the truth, we come to see that what we once perceived as our ultimate capacity was, but a mirage fashioned by self-limitation.

Learning to let go of these constraints is akin to the butterfly letting go of the cocoon. It isn't an act of denial, but rather an embrace of potentiality. There is, therefore, an opportunity for deconstruction where there is courage to confront the barriers constructed in chambers of the mind, untangling the web of thoughts that bind, and making way for a spirit unbridled.

When we acknowledge the fear but choose to act in defiance of it, we find ourselves in the throes of growth. It isn't painless, for the chrysalis of self-imposed limitations does not fall away softly. It requires effort, a deliberate push against the confines of habit and history. In pushing, we become stronger—our resilience against these once-impenetrable barriers grows firmer.

But how do we begin? How do we even identify the invisible walls that we have so carefully built around ourselves? It starts with asking yourself questions and journeying deep into our being, self-inquiry that for too long we have dodged. It means scrutinizing the narratives we've accepted, challenging the status quo of our internal governance, and daring to redraft the constitution of our self-belief.

Inquiries lights up the secret places of our fears and insecurities become lightened, sitting quietly trying to understand them we slowly realize that they don't run us. The process is not a path of linear progression but a dance—one moment forward, another perhaps back, but always a movement towards liberation.

With each step towards freedom, the encumbrances loom less intimidating. They begin to appear like aged scars rather open wounds - testimonies towards where we've been yet not indicators of where we must go. It shapes our path without dictating the direction, pushing us towards a self-discovery more profound to be described only as liberating.

The emergence from our self-imposed encasements brings with it the air of the new—a breath so different in its freshness that every cell within us recognizes the shift. In this space, possibilities once shrouded by our own hands come shimmering into the light. What we dream we also dare; what we envision becomes our endeavor.

It is important to embrace the beauty in the blossoming of ourselves, to not rush through the moments of struggle that accompany the shedding of old, restrictive skins. In the effort, as with the butterfly, there was grace, in the unfolding, magnificence. And it is only through that laborious act of breaking free that at last we may stretch our wings, test them in the light of day, and set ourselves to the flights which we have yet to attempt.

To soar, we need not be fearless—only brave enough to acknowledge the fear and yet move through it. This is how the constraints become but a memory—a tale of what was, not what will be. And as we launch ourselves into the beyond, the uncertainty that might have once made us hesitate becomes the fuel of our ascent.

It is then we soar, on wings unbounded by the shadows of the past. The sky, once an unreachable vista, opens its arms to us with an embrace as wide as our newfound freedom. In the transcendent arc of flight, we understand that our potential is not a fixed star but an entire galaxy—an ever-expanding universe within, waiting to be explored.

The constraints we break are not just chains but chrysalids. What emerges is more glorious than its prior encasement could ever contain. As we rise on the updrafts of our courage and will, it's evident that the only true limitations that ever existed were the ones we placed upon ourselves. In our journey toward unfettered heights, we become the embodiment of the butterfly—the symbol of transformation, resilience, and a boundless spirit surrendered to the winds of change.

The Liberating Experience of Self-Discovery

Emerging from the chrysalis of our previous reflections, let's explore the liberation that is born from the deeply intimate process of self-discovery. For, just as so the butterfly that discovers its wings only after already bound by its cocoon, do we find inside the trials and tribulations of the passage of our life that there is much talent abiding deep within. For, so often we are likened to a little insect before it opens up its four frail wings and decides to lift itself off of the ground for the first time.

Self-discovery is no trivial quest; it is a rich and demanding journey that calls for introspection and honesty. It's swimming through the depths of our past, present, and potential. It's swimming through the depths of our past, present, and potential. Just as the butterfly must trust in its instinct to go liquid within the cocoon, we must trust that inner wisdom will guide us through the valleys and peaks of understanding who we truly are.

So, peeling back the layers of our identity- doing so in discomfort. Yet within this discomfort lies the seed of growth. Our identity are not monoliths but mosaics complex and colorful built from every experience, every triumph and yes every scar. While we face our fear and embrace our truth, we're shedding the constraints of who were though that we had to be and beginning to accept who in facts we are

Consider for a moment the sheer wonder a butterfly might perceive as it tests its newfound wings. The limitless sky, once an impossible dream within the dark enclosure of the cocoon, now beckons with the promise of uncharted voyages. Similarly, when we commit to learning about ourselves, we unlock a realm of infinite possibilities, a breath of potential that can carry us to new horizons.

Personal liberation after self-discovery is not just about understanding one's preferences or acknowledging strengths and weaknesses. It's a fuller, deeper understanding that allows one to make peace with his or her imperfections and celebrate the unique composition that is 'self'. It's attuning to one's values, a harmony with one's very own rhythm in the symphony of life.

We should never forget that self-discovery also means exploring our relationships with others, with our environment, and with the world at large. Just as the waves made by the movement of its new wings in the air, the butterfly's newfound identity influences its surrounds – its actions – and can influence a change in those it touches.

To embark on this journey is to let go of pretense and to embrace vulnerability. It can be an unsettling experience, as the roots of our being are shaken free from the soil of security. But it is within this upheaval that we unearth our genuine selves, resilient and raw in their beauty.

As we walk the paths of self-discovery, shadows may be discovered amongst the light-parts of us to which we have not paid attention or that we've quieted. Unacknowledged wounds and unresolved stories all live in the shadows waiting for their day in the sun. Our challenge is to illuminate these darker patches with the same warmth and acceptance we grant our more apparent qualities.

Remember that the process of self-discovery unfolds in its own time. There will be times that you think that you are lost and floating around in an ocean of the unknown. But every time that you take a deeper dive and travel further and further out to sea, you are making a way towards freedom.

Much as a butterfly needs time for its wings to dry before taking to the air, we too need the process of discovery of who we are through recognizing downtime for relaxation, to digest information, and for contemplation before making the needful discoveries. It is only natural that we need us time to passively absorb information and let it sink in.

The process of self-discovery would have taught us to establish limits and to say "no" as easily as "yes." Once clouded by insecurity and the expectations of others, today we see clearly and are far better equipped to negotiate life. We infuse every forward step with the power of true self-expression into choices which are reflective of our innermost wants.

The butterfly teaches us that there is grace in the search for the self, that each flutter of wings and beat of heart contributes to the journey.

It is not a race, but a lifelong expedition where the treasure lies in the lessons gleaned and the personal victories achieved.

To discover oneself is to construct a map where 'X' marks the current moment, dotted lines trace where we've been, and vast blank spaces anticipate the adventures yet to come. It's the recognition that we are works in progress and that every iteration, every version of ourselves, deserves celebration.

On the highest summits of self-awareness, we do experience an breathtaking panoramic view of our lives from new angles. It's a challenging landscape where every peak conquered contributes to make the experience of existence more breathtaking. We see that life's tapestry is richer for our participation, vibrantly woven with threads of our individual experiences.

And so, as that passage though self-discovery comes to a close, we stand at the precipice of our potential gazing out at the vast expanse of sky that awaits. And thus, with the wind of understanding under our wings we shall take off the earth and fly above the area of constrains into the world grasping it in the knowledge of what we really are.

Chapter 7:
Navigating Storms: Finding Calm Amidst Chaos

Within the cycle of life, storms are inevitable, much like the butterfly which, despite its fragility, must occasionally brave the tempest's fury. This chapter rests on the precipice of turmoil, peering into the swirling maelstrom of life's trials while seeking the silent heartbeat of tranquility within. Here, we wade through the tempestuous climates, not unscathed but undeterred, mirroring the butterfly's resilience against nature's capricious wrath. Through stories that echo the flutter of delicate wings against the fierce winds, we'll explore the innate capacity to discover peace amidst chaos. One dives into the peaceful depths of meditation and awareness, those psychotic refuges within the citadel of the soul where calm reigns for a time in spite of the outward turmoil. It is in this very heart of the storm that we will find peace, that haven that will enable us not to just rub along but to flourish as all about us gets into turmoil.

Discussing the Storms Butterflies Endure During Their Life Cycle

Unfurling narratives of resilience and transformation, I turn from the creature with the least power on my list to that most delicate yet remarkably enduring of creatures: the butterfly. From the literal and metaphorical storms these creatures endure throughout this life cycle, lift the curtain on profound truths about existence. Through the lives of these fleeting marvels, we gain insight into the tempests that buffet us, humans, and how, like the butterfly, we might emerge from the turmoil with grace.

Consider the caterpillar, enshrined in its chrysalis, as not merely a prelude, but a brave soul weathering the first of its life's torrents. The creature's transformation within this silken chamber is nothing short of a tempest. Cells break down, structures dissolve, all while the capsule sways in the wind. This is a storm of the self, a necessary upheaval for growth. It's a stark reminder that our internal battles, our moments of breaking down, are cornerstones upon which we build our future selves.

The emergence of the butterfly is not simply a dawn of new form, but also an introduction to the volatility of the skies. The butterfly's maiden flight might be met with the battering winds of adversity. Wings, damp and soft, must harden quickly to rise above the gusts that seek to ground new potential. So too must we, in the fresh stages of transformation, prepare to endure the buffeting of life's unforeseen challenges.

As butterflies navigate through their existence, storms, both unexpected and inevitable, mark the terrain of their flight paths. Even with the most vibrant of wings, rain lashes, disrupting the aerodynamics of their flight. In these moments, resilience is the silent beat keeping them aloft. They must persevere, a testament to the strength within delicate frames; a strength that we, too, possess inherently.

Do not underestimate the butterfly's awareness of when to seek shelter, to rest and wait for the storm to pass. These periods of pause are natural, an understanding that endurance is not a perpetual battle against the elements, but an art of knowing when to hold fast until calm skies return. In life's maelstrom, we too can find solace in stillness, learning to trust in the moments of reprieve.

While some butterflies fold their wings against the driving rain, others take to the winds with a tenacious spirit. They ride the currents, using the forces that might well overcome them as means to propel forward. Their plight teaches us that sometimes adversity can be channeled into a powerful ally, pushing us further than we envisioned we could travel.

Throughout its life, the butterfly witnesses the changing of the seasons—each bringing a different tempest to bear. From spring showers to summer heatwaves, and the harrowing chill of autumn winds, adaptation is not just an instinct, it's a crafted skill. As individuals, our lives are similarly marked by seasons of change: some fertile, others barren, yet all part of an ever-evolving pattern.

The life of a butterfly is a tapestry woven with trials, threaded with episodes of fragility and resilience in equal measure. They survive predators, shortages of food, and environmental extremities. We too face predators of the spirit, scarcities of hope, and climates of societal pressures. Yet, we persist and often thrive, driven by the same powerful instinct to endure.

What becomes clear in observing the life of the butterfly is that every storm, regardless of its severity, has an end. And often, in the wake of the gale, the world is brighter, flowers are thirstier for the touch of the butterfly, and life itself seems to lean forward in anticipation of the caress of wingtips. So too does our human spirit rejoice in the aftermath of difficulty, often finding the newfound strength that had been forged in the crucible of challenge.

Consider the butterfly who lands, for just a moment, upon a boisterous child's hand. The storm that is human playfulness poses no small threat to such a fragile being. And yet, it stays, unflinching—a lesson in the courage to face towering giants and emerge unscathed, in finding tranquility amidst chaos.

In their final days, butterflies embody the pinnacle of resilience. Their bodies are weary, wings tattered from the countless storms weathered, yet they continue to seek nectar and to dance in the sunlight. It is a reminder to us that, even when worn by time and toil, joy and purpose should fuel our days until the very end.

As the butterfly's journey comes full circle, its offspring—tiny eggs clinging to a leaf—will soon begin their own saga of weathering life's tempests. It is a cycle that perpetuates the species, and a metaphor for the generational resilience that we embed in our own progeny through the stories we share and the examples we set.

The storm element is only referred to indirectly as one part alluding to the vulnerability and vigor imprinted in the eternal lessons gleaned from the transition from caterpillar into to a winged wanderer with quick transitions. In each flutter against the squall, there echoes a story of survival, a harmonious symphony that plays a familiar tune to our human hearts.

In facing life's unending gales, may we recall the wingbeats of the butterfly that whipped against the tempest, yet continued its delicate dance upon the air. Their journey parallel to our own—each turn in the storm a chance to catch the wind, to rise again, to find the calm amidst chaos, and to remember that life's truest beauty may be found not despite the tempests, but because of them.

Our destinies are not unlike these fragile wanderers of the sky. With each storm comes an opportunity to demonstrate our strength, embrace the winds of change, and perhaps, above all, find exaltation in the magnificent voyage that is life.

Providing Insights on Finding Inner Peace and Calmness During Life's Challenges

Turmoil in the luminous dance of life erupts suddenly as does a summer storm. The elusive sanctuary. Inner peace. Just as the butterfly masters the winds of a tempest, we too must learn the art of finding calm within chaos. The journey to such tranquility within is not just a fluke; it is a conscious one that requires self-reflection and being in touch with what lies deeper in ourselves.

Visualize, if you will, the butterfly, gently flitting from leaf to leaf, unwavering even as the winds howl. It is not a piece of stillness but a calm on the inside that shouts louder than all the noise in this world. Likewise, when the storms of life are raging madly about us, we contact a peace which is outside this physical world. Embarking on this quest demands that we first acknowledge the storms we cannot control.

Accepting this lack of control is not an act of defeat but a bold step towards mastering our inner landscape. By taking the time to sort through the thoughts and emotions with the tender loving care of a gardener, the underbrush of disorderly tangles may slowly be weeded out of one's stream of consciousness.

It helps to close one's eyes and envision the chaos as waves crashing against the sturdy rocks of our consciousness. Though the water may thrash, it can't erode what is eternally steadfast within us. With each breath, we become more like those enduring stones, able to withstand the torrents without losing pieces of ourselves to the tide.

Tranquility can be cultivated with the practice of mindfulness, a way of being thoroughly present to the quality of your life, moment by moment. Just like butterflies enjoy nectar of every flower it alights on, mindfulness requires we experience moments without resistance or distraction. Pouring our all into the present stills tomorrow's anxious and melts yesterday's echoes, to make space peace to bloom.

Meditation, too, serves as a beacon through the fog of our troubles. We can hear the whispers of our inner voice guiding us towards equanimity, in the silence of meditation. Just as the butterfly lands daintily on a petal, taking pause to settle herself before she pieces the air with her flight again, so does meditation offer us that same still silence where our restless flight through life can come to rest just for a moment as peace lands softly on our shoulders.

Another gateway to calmness is through the embodiment of gratitude. By focusing on the abundance in our lives, we shift attention away from the tumult and towards the blessings that are as numerous as the stars. Each instance of thankfulness is akin to a gentle flap of the butterfly's wings, creating ripples that stir up joy and dispel the clouds of disquiet.

Finding inner peace also requires us to foster fingers with both the natural world as well as people around us. Nature, in all its resplendent glory speaks a language stillness that soothes the soul. And in the eyes of another, we can find reflections of our shared humanity that transcend the upheaval. These connections anchor us; they remind us that we are not alone in our battles against the storms.

This should be a very important consideration of self-compassion during the process of finding inner peace. Like how the butterfly does not resist the amount of time within the wrapping of a cocoon, one should not blame on themselves how long it will take them to find peace within adversity.

Our journey may be fraught with trials, yet with each act of kindness we show ourselves, we step closer to a profound serenity.

Remember, within us resides a wellspring of strength; it's the same potency that allows the butterfly to emerge from the cocoon anew. This inner fortitude helps us face life's challenges without capitulating to disorder. It is a whisper of courage when shadows loom, a beacon of hope when the night seems endless.

Let's learn to flow in the moments of silence as we weave through life's wonderful challenges. During this interval, we can reflect on our path, recharge our soul, and reconnect with our core. In these interludes, we can reflect on our path, recharge our spirits, and realign with our core. These moments are as essential as the butterfly's stops along its migration – each one an opportunity to gather energy and clarity for the journey ahead.

And so, within the folds of our beings, let us fashion a sanctuary of peace. We must remind ourselves that, much like the butterfly, our transformation is continuous and often birthed from the heart of chaos itself. It's within this transformation that tranquility is not just found but also created, an ever-present force, akin to the silent grace of a butterfly's glide through the storm.

In this gift of life, where tumult is as certain as the rising sun, we do not search for a world without wind. Instead, we seek the strength to unfurl our wings, to find the current that will carry us through. With each flap, every struggle, and all the striving, peace becomes not a distant dream, but a reality we enact, a calm that we embody, a grace we live, moment by breathless moment.

May we all find that steady place within, where storms may rage, but peace remains untouched.

Mindfulness and Meditation Techniques for Navigating Through Turbulent Times

In the journey through life's tempests, there lies a quiet strength within the embrace of mindfulness and meditation—techniques that whisper of ancient wisdom and modern science in equal measure. Like the butterfly that must weather violent rains and gusty winds, humans too seek solace amidst the chaos of their internal and external worlds. Herein we traverse methods of calming the spirit, aligning the psyche, and transforming our very essence through the gentle power of mindful presence and meditative contemplation.

Mindfulness as we imagine it here involves bringing attention to experiences happening in the present moment without being judgmental. Imagine sitting still and observing the metamorphosis that a caterpillar experiences. Such quietness evokes clarity, as if each breath we take allows us to perceive the subtle hues and delicate textures of life's intricate design. Similarly, mindfulness enables us to observe our thoughts and emotions as they are—mere fluttering wings in the vast sky of our consciousness.

To initiate this practice, one might simply find a quiet corner, a haven of tranquility akin to the protective silk of a chrysalis. Here, seated comfortably or lying down, with eyes closed or softly focused, we begin to turn inward. Attention is gently guided to the breath—a natural anchor to the present—and maintained with the effortless grace of a butterfly's glide.

Meditation is, mind you, is interwoven with mindfulness much of the time yet takes us farther indeed into the heart of stillness. It is an intentional turning away from the clamor of the swarm, a travel to the center of one's being. There are various meditative practices, much like the diverse species of butterflies, each with its unique vibrancy and pattern. Some methods involve concentration, mindfully focusing on an object, sound, or even the act of walking. Others embrace contemplation or the chanting of mantras, their resonance reminiscent of the gentle flapping of wings against the silence of the air.

In times of stress and uncertainty, the breath can serve as a sacred refuge, a rhythmic reminder of life's undulating pulse. The focus becomes all about the inhalation and exhalation that the walls of anxiety seem to melt away and in its place is a fort of peace built with each realized breath. On every drawn breath we become aware of how to hurdle that which hurts ourselves as we simply release anxieties and fears like a butterfly prematurely let go of its cocoon.

Body scan meditation is another technique, inviting us to attend to each part of our physical form, from the tips of our toes to the crown of our heads. It is a reverent acknowledgment of our corporeal existence, an exploration of the vessel that carries us through our tumultuous journey. With tender and patient awareness, we come to accept our bodies as they are, strong yet vulnerable, a paradox echoing the delicate strength of a butterfly's wings.

Loving-kindness meditation enlarges our anxious concern, urging us to extend well-wishing into ourselves and others. It is a meditation that embraces all of life's interdependence, much akin to the scene of air-currents which obstruct and support a butterfly's flight. Here, we nurture our inherent capacity for compassion, finding in our hearts the ability to soar above spite and malice.

Mindfulness and meditation also offer sanctuary amidst the storms through visualization. Envisioning oneself in a place of serenity—be it a serene garden filled with iridescent wings or the rugged beauty of a mountain peak—can serve as an inner retreat. These mental landscapes become a backdrop against which we paint our calm, imbuing ourselves with a sense of ease and comfort against life's buffering torrents.

Grounding techniques, akin to the rootedness of the caterpillar before its ascent, remind us of our connection to the Earth. By simply walking barefoot on the grass or sand, we tether our restless spirits to the dependable solidity of the ground below, drawing strength and stability from our Mother Earth. This physical anchoring can alleviate the chaos that storms within, offering a powerful counterbalance to mental and emotional turbulence.

Journaling—weaving words into a tapestry of reflection—can also echo the practice of mindfulness. Just as a butterfly leaf fleeting trails of beauty in its wake, similarly, writing down one's emotions and ideas can serve as a record of his path onto self-awareness and acceptance. It is an introspective talk with oneself, digging the deepest darkest corners and highest ambitious being of the psyche.

Mantra repetition offers a lifeline when waves crash and thunder roars. A simple phrase, repeated with intention and focus, can still the quivering heart and stabilize the erratic mind. Each syllable hums with vibrational energy, a lullaby for the spirit that soothes and comforts, much like the reassuring presence of the sun behind the sternest of clouds.

Gratitude practices, the acknowledgment of blessings both grand and minute, can shift perspectives radically. When we focus our awareness on the gifts nestled within the struggles—the learning, the growth, the sheer miracle of existence—our burdens are transmuted into wings upon which we rise. Such is the transformative potential of a grateful heart, basking in the warmth of life's myriad offerings.

Even beyond these techniques, merely paying attention in a mindful way when you eat, move or listen becomes a portable meditation. A strand of gold that catches the ephemeral sunlight like a butterfly landing on a sun-kissed blossom is presence; it's the thread that weaves through our days. It is the full embodiment of each moment, a resplendent tableau of the here and now.

Mindfulness and meditation, these twin pillars of peace, stand resolute as the storms of circumstance rage about us. They are the sanctuary for the soul, teachings that transcend time and speak to the heart of human experience. And just as the butterfly skims the turbulence created by the life-giving winds, finding hope in the very movement that otherwise impels it to disaster, we sometimes need to embrace the turbulence caused by the problems in our respective lives, realizing of course that at our core is an innate reservoir of strength and resiliency that will see us through - to come out on the other side, transformed and ready to be on wing.

May the techniques outlined in this timeless interlude serve you well as you journey through your own storms and emerge, not merely unscathed, but renewed and resplendent, ready to soar to newfound heights with grace and poise.

Chapter 8:
Spread Your Wings - Practical Strategies

Having navigated the tumultuous climates of our inner world, we arrive at a juncture where knowledge must be shaped into action. Considering and using everything we have learned thus far, this chapter describes substantive methods with which to formulate a very individual plan for change that is just so singular as the pattern on a butterfly's wing. It reminds us that efforts need to be fortified like perfect wings as of a lepidopteran, about to emerge from its cocoon.

We will explore ways to create your individual growth plan, echoing the precision seen in nature, fueling your resolve to rise above former limitations and glide towards your aspirations. Each strategy is a thread in the cocoon, binding your metamorphosis with purposeful intent. Wisdom lies not where beauty is. It certainly doesn't with a butterfly that would eternally be caught up in the roving ruckus of its psychopathic memory, but instead, our true worth will be in the multilayered quality of persistence, courage, and dreams we'll try to stitch into the frayed disarray called life.

Practical Steps for Personal Transformation

Transformation is not just the ability to put away old skin, but a conscious process of growing into who we are meant to become. As it is with butterflies, the process that goes from cocoon to flight isn't a crap shoot; it's an evolutionary process, a sequence of delicate steps that converge and result with the animal opening up its wings.

Likewise, personal transformation requires actionable efforts, a steady progression towards the brilliance of being our truest selves.

First and foremost, start with where you are at in your life now. When it is time to emerge like the butterfly who knows when instinctively, understand the realms emotionally, physically and mentally great and small change is needed. Acknowledge without judgment the areas that need nurturing and commit to growth. This self-awareness is the dawn of transformation.

Construct a vision for your life that mirrors the clarity and singularity of purpose that propels a butterfly from its cocoon. Define what personal success and happiness mean to you. Let that vision be vivid, adorned with the colors of your most passionate inclinations and aspirations, much like the intricate patterns on a butterfly's wings. This vision will be the compass that guides your steps.

The path to transformation is paved with intentions, so set goals that are not just lofty but also tangible. Minor changes accumulated over time create a composite of significant transformation. Set these goals like milestones along a journey, achievable, challenging, yet exciting—something to strive towards with zeal and consistency.

Transformation demands courage. Take a step away from the seeming safety of what you've always known and learn to embrace the discomfort of the unknown. Just as the butterfly must fight out of its cocoon to strengthen its wings, so also should you when faced with all challenges because it is the forge upon which resilience and strength for flight are tempered.

Alongside setting goals, institute daily rituals that build the discipline you need. Whether it's rising with the sun to meditate, dedicating time for reading and learning, or pursuing physical fitness, each ritual contributes to the robustness of your wings. To transform, one must harmonize the forces of mind, body, and spirit.

Personal transformation is inextricably linked with letting go. Just as the butterfly breaks out of its cocoon, so also must your own self-limiting doubt, self-inadequacy beliefs and fears. Go deeply into the stories that you have told yourself about your limits and re-write them with possibility and resolve.

Learn from the world around you as much you can through the stories of those who have gone before you, from the stillness of nature and from the limitless expanse of literature and philosophy.

In wisdom, find the nectar that fuels growth, much like the sustenance a butterfly finds in flowers.

Cultivate the art of patience. Each stage in the journey of the butterfly is a testament to the power of patient endeavor. Know that transformation cannot be rushed. Give yourself the grace to evolve at a pace that allows each lesson to imbue its essence into your being.

Reflection is an essential asset in this metamorphosis. Reflect upon each day with the gentle scrutiny of one who seeks to grow. Contemplate your actions, emotions, and reactions, learning from each with the wisdom of one who understands that every experience is a thread in the tapestry of personal evolution.

Connection is at the heart of a butterfly's existence—without it, the tapestry of nature would fray. So too must you connect—with those around you, with the environment, with the experiences that knit into the narrative of your life's tale. Surround yourself with a community of practice that lifts your dreams, shares your vision, and that supports your transformational experience.

Be strong as the storms will come as an ally that gives strength. Be like those butterflies who dance in the rain, learning to take strength from adversity. Cultivate having grit, that intangible quality that makes you press forward, even when the winds of challenge howl meanly with frustration.

In your quest for transformation, practice gratitude. Acknowledge the beauty of the process, the people who aid your journey, and even the struggles that shape your strength. Because gratitude has a power to turn an ordinary day into a whole mosaic of happiness and joy, just as simple beauty makes a butterfly spread its wings and meet the dawn.

As you implement these practical steps, remember that personal transformation is not a destination but a journey—a continuous process of becoming, of reaching for heights yet unattained, of spreading your wings in bold and vivid defiance of the gravity that once held you earthbound. Carry forth with the knowledge that within you lies the potential for wondrous metamorphosis.

Lastly, let go of the expectation for immediate change. A butterfly does not emerge fully formed; it grows into its colors and wingspan with time. Allow yourself the same natural progression, and in doing so, find the courage to spread your wings and take the flight of transformation.

From that cocoon of self-doubt, emerging through these practical steps, to liberation in self-realization, may yours be a journey filled with growth and resilience and beauty that one cannot adequately appreciate — until you are the butterfly figure.

Creating a Personal Growth Plan

As we journey further, think of yourself as a cartographer mapping uncharted territories. You are both the map and the compass. Your personal growth plan is not merely an itinerary, it's an act of hope—a declaration that you have the power to evolve, much like our butterfly who emerges transformed. Composing this plan is an intimate process, where soul speaks to paper, and wishes ink themselves into clear, attainable goals.

The inception of your transformative plan, begin with self-reflection. Just stop for a while because the world keeps on revolving while we never stop to breathe just once. In this silence, dear yourself where are you and what lies into the abyss of your desires. Establishment of your objectives is a sacred ritual. It needs to touch you where it hurts, stir up emotions that may have been buried under the weight of daily life. The colors of a butterfly's wings represent the wide range of possible aspirations; they can be as simple as climbing the corporate ladder or as complex as finding contentment within yourself.

Nestled within this planning, the understanding of your current resources is crucial. Assess your strengths as one would admire the sturdiness and patterns of wings; these are your tools to navigate the vast skies. Examine your limitations—not as hindrances but as the winds that compel you to soar higher. You must know your essence inside out, as the butterfly knows each cell that constructs its form.

Let the metamorphosis of goals into action plans begin. Chart the steps you must undertake—no step too minuscule, no stride too ambitious. The path may twist and coil unexpectedly, mimic the erratic flutter of a butterfly, but even the most whimsical flight follows a pattern only known to its wielder. Map the milestones, for each one will be a testament to your progress, much as each flap of the butterfly's wings propels it forward.

Your plan should be inked with accountability—delicately lace it with deadlines, for a plan without a time frame remains but a dream. The butterfly's transformation adheres to nature's unwritten calendar, and so shall your growth observe the boundaries set by self-imposed timelines, yet with the gentleness of the morning's first light.

Preparation for adversity is not pessimism but the wisdom of the meadow, where the butterfly knows the promise of rain as much as it does the warmth of the sun. Equip your plan with contingency strategies. What shall you do when the wind resists or storms assail? Resilience, much admired in nature's winged beauties, shall also be your cloak and shield.

Pledging to a personal growth plan is a solemn vow to oneself. Commitment weaves the chrysalis; it is the tender yet tensile thread upon which transformation balances. Determine how you will measure growth and success. Will it be through tangible outcomes or the more abstract evolution of your being? Choose your metrics as the butterfly chooses the flower—instinctively, wisely.

Amidst the pursuit of objectives lies the irreplaceable requirement for self-compassion. Err you might, falter you may, as even the most graceful butterfly momentarily loses its dance to wayward winds. Forgive yourself for the missteps and treasure them. They are not failures but simply steps in another rhythm, propelling your flight anew.

Intertwine your growth with the growth of others; let it not be a solitary voyage. Much like our butterfly which pollinates as it partakes in nectar, let your journey aid fellow sojourners. Serve as the breeze that uplifts others, share your discoveries, and learn from theirs. Community is the garden where an individual's flower blooms in unison.

Review and revisitation of your growth plan are as mandatory as the need for the butterfly to rest its wings. Periodically alight from your flight, reflect on how far the winds have carried you, realign with your compass if you must. Transformation is malleable, and your plan must embrace the fluidity of life's continuous ebb and tide.

Surround your endeavor with mentors, human guideposts, who resemble the sun's position for the butterfly—providing direction and warmth. Seek wisdom from those who've journeyed before you, harness their experiences as you would the warm currents that support the butterfly's ascent. Cultivate relationships that challenge and champion your progress.

Documentation of your personal growth odyssey is both a task and a treasure. Maintain a journal, a log of thoughts, emotions, and achievements. Like the dust on a butterfly's wings, each entry is a unique fragment of the journey, containing the magic of your narrative. Let it be a legacy of your passage through time, a tale told with pride.

The fluidity of your plan must mirror the incessant motion of life. Welcome the unexpected, the unplanned detours that life invariably presents. The beauty of the butterfly's flight is in its unpredictability and in its faith in the winds. Your plan's capacity to adapt is congruent with the butterflies to the ever-changing environment.

To conclude, your personal growth plan is your covenant with destiny, woven from the threads of your deepest aspirations and ironclad in your will to achieve them. Let it flutter beside you—your silent ally—as you explore the vastness of your potential. Let it guide you through storms, past the horizon, towards the tranquil yet vibrant meadows of your dreams.

Integrating Lessons from the Butterfly into Daily Life

In the quietude of self-reflection, we can gather the threads of wisdom spun from the butterfly's tapestry. Like a colorful winged creature delicately poised on the brink of discovery, we embody potential in the nurtured silences of our days. The undertaking lies in weaving these threads into the fabric of our daily existence.

Just as a butterfly emerges with wings that vibrantly affirm life, we, too, can step gracefully into our routines, bearing the sheen of our learned experiences. It begins with the simple act of intention—rise each day with a resolve as steadfast as the rising sun that warms a butterfly's wings; awaken with a purpose that fuels your flight.

Mornings offer opportunities for metamorphosis. Embrace the day's predictability but infuse it with the ingenuity of transformation. Whether it means altering your commute to rekindle curiosity or challenging your mind with a new book during breakfast, let the mundane serve as a canvas for your own innovation and growth.

Throughout the day, molten moments may harden into challenges. Recall the resilience of the butterfly, braving winds, and weather; its grace belies the sheer vigorous adaptation beneath its wings. Allow yourself to adapt, to be pliable and powerful, cheerful in the face of adversity, and as tenacious as life itself.

In the pulse of interaction, remember that your words flutter out like wings, touching others with gentleness or force. Speak kindness and truth, for your conversations can pollinate minds with new thoughts, just as the butterfly cross-pollinates the blooms that slip quietly across its path.

The noon of our lives can blaze with relentless intensity, tempting us to seek the solace of shadows. Yet, in this zenith of activity, discover a moment to elevate your perspective. Briefly close your eyes, envision a butterfly's panoramic view, and let this vision realign your priorities with what truly uplifts your soul.

As evenings drape their calming shroud, reflect on the progression from cocoon to flight, and from strife to gratifying calm. Acknowledge the toil behind the apparent ease. Your strides, no less remarkable than a butterfly's first flutter, merit equal reverence and recognition.

Laced within our meals, whether sumptuous or spare, lies the nectar of gratitude. Taste your food as a butterfly tastes the sweetness in each flower, wholly immersed in the moment—savor the joy of the present, here, now, always.

As dusk welcomes stars that herald the moon, plant seeds of joy as unfalteringly as a butterfly that alights from flower to flower. Let your actions be deliberate and meaningful, supportive of the growth you wish to see in yourself and in the lives touched by your presence.

Our lives are scored in silence and serenity, much akin to the hush of twilight hours. Engage in quiet contemplation like the butterfly at rest, poised and peaceful, gathering strength for the morrow. Employ meditation, prayer, or reflection to connect with the core of your being.

Unseen to most are the storms weathered by delicate wings; acknowledge your personal tempests and stand resilient. Draw courage and comfort in the knowledge that storms strengthen, sculpt, and refine. Each trial navigated grants you clearer skies, just as clear days follow the butterfly's storm.

Our nights are harbors of dreams, akin to cocoons where metamorphosis unfolds unseen. Cherish your dreams as sacred spaces where you can be reborn each night, your aspirations as chrysalides awaiting the warmth of a new day's resolve.

To love and be loved form the bedrock of existence. As the butterfly nurtures harmony within the environment, build relationships that exude warmth, trust, and mutual nourishment. Your emotional bonds are destinies intertwined, roots and wings entwined.

Each dawn marks the continuation of your journey. Move forward with an unwavering cadence towards the light of your highest self, just as the butterfly, instinctual, endeavors towards sunlit paths. Though the flight paths may change, your true north is constant, guiding your journey ever upward, ever outward.

Finally, at each day's culmination, as you settle into the sanctuary of sleep, forgive. Forgive yourself and others, much as the butterfly, unencumbered by yesteryears, takes to the skies in persistent pursuit of life's boundless beauties. Embrace the cycle of rest and awakening as gateways to infinite possibilities.

In these ways—through intention, adaptation, kindness, fortitude, gratitude, serenity, resilience, dreaming, loving, forgiving—we don't just integrate the lessons of the butterfly; we honor them. We allow them to take root within us, to unfold in brilliant splashes of lived color, and to teach us that ours is a life of continuous blossoming, an unfolding iridescence that is crafted, day by intricately woven day.

Chapter 9:
Cultivate a Garden of Joy

As we traverse further into our journey, akin to the butterfly alighting from flower to flower, we find ourselves in a space bathed in golden sunlight, the air thick with the scent of blooming aspirations—it's here we pause to cultivate our own garden of joy. The colorful wings of each butterfly as it's soft-landing touches life giving flowers sowing seeds of beauty and creating a symphony wide across the planet. It's a gentle reminder that our own moments of happiness spread their roots in the rich soil of present experiences, nurtured by the delicate touch of our interactions. To be joyful is keeping the attitude of genuine satisfaction, building relationships that give the spirit up-lift, giving value to every little thing in life with an exultant heart who has enough not just for pleasures that are sought for fleetingly. In this chapter, let us guide our minds to revel in mindful waters, to embrace the flourishing tendrils of lighthearted connections, and to cultivate a wellspring of joy that not only sustains us but allows us to thrive amidst the tapestry of existence.

Connecting with the Joy of Being

Lonely, solitary flutters by as peer into the boundless of sky—the single butterfly, with sunlit wings kissed gently in their journey. From which flows pure, untamed delight—one cannot deny it from that it from it pours a completion of life's simplest and yet profoundest state—joy. To connect with the joy of being is much like the butterfly's role in the garden, vital and constantly revitalizing.

In all we do, joy can be remote, elusive treasure and sometimes high up on a shelf. Still, in our own lives, with the busy-ness of our all, as with the butterfly who stops to sip from flitting blossoms, we must slow down some, let the moments of peace and happiness come land upon our hearts.

The joy of being thrives on presence—a mindful immersion in the now. Amid the rush, it whispers, soft yet insistent. To hear it, we might turn to the world outside our windows, where life unfolds in unhurried rhythms. The universe offers many possibilities for an individual to experience the essence of peaceful and joy, such as the harmonic song of birds at dawn, the elegance of a butterfly when it flies, and the swinging of trees in the breeze which we often don't pay attention to.

We feel this ecstasy through the intricate choreography of life. Great deeds and successes, as a rule, stay unnoticeable and don't materialize in an everyday life with small, inconspicuous aspects but still very important - as well as in the pauses between separate days. For example, sensory stimulation for instance the soft touch of the sun rays on our skin, the sound that a friend can make when in joy, or a book that truly touches our lives to the core. It is a metaphor of metamorphosis, which encompasses the early unripe stages, following grown-up ones and final release in butterfly's life cycle. Living with a composed determination, and embracing life exemplify the strength that one can gain when being open and susceptible despite challenges experienced by him or her.

We are reminded that the essence of joy is not the absence of pain but the celebration of survival, the finding of light in shadows.

In a world that often prizes the tangible and the quantifiable, the joy of being is ethereal, slippery—an art form unto itself. It requires an intention to cultivate, a garden that needs tending. We must weed out the hurry that chokes and choose instead to plant seeds of mindfulness, watching them blossom into moments of sheer bliss.

This inherent joy transcends circumstances; it is not a destination but a manner of traveling. Like the butterfly that moves from flower to flower, radiating beauty and expedites a purpose larger than itself, in the same way can we become dispensers of joys into our private lives as well as the lives we intersect.

How do we sustain this delicate joy in times of adversity? We look again to our winged companions, who, against the odds, remain undeterred by the coming storm. Their resilience is as inherent as their grace, a pattern for our own hearts to follow. Despite winds that may bend us, we remain rooted in our capacity for joy.

The communal dance between the butterfly and the bloom is a powerful reminder that our joy often echoes in the shared experiences with others. Every genuine smile, every compassionate gesture, every act of kindness nurtures the joy that connects our spirits like invisible threads weaving through the tapestry of humanity.

And so, as we trek through the varied terrain of our lives, let us enshrine moments of pure joy within us. These brief encounters with bliss are more than mere memories—they are the pulse of our existence, the hum that underscores our essence.

To be in a state of joy is not to cling to transitory pleasures, but to cultivate an inner sanctuary of peace—a sanctum that weathers the world's changing tide. This internal haven is where we retreat to find solace, to recharge, to emerge with quiet strength like the butterfly after a storm.

We each have a choice, a daily decision to be architects of our joy. It beckons us to look beyond life's superficialities, to connect deeply with our being. Each mindful step, each breath drawn in awareness is a deliberate act of creating the garden where our joy can flourish.

As our narrative weaves forward, remember the butterfly's silent lesson. Its dance in the wind is not just a beacon of transformation but an ode to the joy that life offers freely. May we embrace this invitation with wide open arms and a willing heart, to alight upon the joy that's ours to claim, ever-present in the garden of our existence.

In the following chapters, we will explore the intricate ways in which butterflies benefit ecosystems and how we can also provide joy to our communities. But in this precious now, let us truly embrace the joy of being, and know that the fragile wings of contentment are inside us, waiting to be let loose. And at the point where our journey culminates, let the joy of being be our compass that guides us through the labyrinth of living reminding us ever to seek out the enchanting in the ordinary, everyday, silent flutter of a butterfly's wing against the wide expanse of life.

The Butterfly's Role in Pollination and Its Connection to Spreading Joy

Like a garden tended with purpose, our inner landscapes are the fertile breeding-grounds for joy much in the same way in which delicate flowers are nudged by the soft meanderings of butterflies. And as we dig further into the humus of our 'Garden of Joy', we would unearth the delicate role that played out for the butterfly. not just a spectator in this garden but its accidental cultivator. Through pollination, these ethereal beings weave a tapestry of life, connecting flower to flower, soul to soul, spreading not only the seeds of flora but of happiness.

The butterfly's wings flutter porous yet start a symphony of motion that will change the very nature of existence. Their flight between blooms, unpretentious in their duty as they savor nectar; also, to ferry pollen to grant life to the waiting embrace of other blossoms. This process is a paragon of nature's interconnectedness—each flutter, a touch, a shared intimacy, a transfer of life's essence from one to another.

In these flights and flutters, there echoes a narrative of shared joy. The blossoms that burst forth are not solitary celebrants; rather, they are the resplendent outcomes of partnerships and communal endeavors. The butterfly, in its role, is a facilitator of connections. Each visitation brings with it the opportunity for new life, for diversity, and for the brightness and beauty that such a fresh canvas of flora can offer.

Contemplate this—each blossom in your garden began as a whisper of potential, much like the inklings of joy in the recesses of your heart. As the butterfly alights upon each, it reaffirms its existence, bestowing the chance to flourish. Pollen grains, under the microscope, are the architects of tomorrow's gardens; so too are our small acts of joy, which become cornerstones of a life more radiant.

The necessity of the butterfly's journey illustrates a fundamental truth in our own lives—the joy we find, and foster is seldom a secluded endeavor. It thrives through our interactions; in the convivial exchanges we share with those around us. Life's pollination comes in the form of smiles shared, kindnesses bestowed, and support offered.

We can place ourselves in roles like that of the butterfly, flitting from one life to another, oblivious of the joy dust we are leaving behind or how we meant something so simple to someone's garden of happiness. There is manifold satisfaction derived from the nectar of our own experiences when we know it adds to the blooming of someone else's dream and aspirations.

The influence of the butterfly is not constrained to the physical realm; it's an endless ripple across the pond of existence. Joy, once seeded, knows no bounds; it spreads with vigor, coloring the world in vibrant hues of bliss, hope, and delight, each shade begetting another.

In the deliberate care of our gardens, we must acknowledge the necessity of butterflies—their role in renewal and in bridging one joy to another. Isn't it remarkable how our happiness, too, when shared, breeds more of its kind? Our laughter, our positive thoughts, our humane spirit—it is the pollen that fertilizes the soulful connections of our lives, germinating legacies of euphoria.

As gardeners of joy, we recognize the symbiotic relationship we share with our environment, how the seeds we sow with love and care return to us manifold. The butterfly does not choose the flower it aids in fruition; it simply lands where it may, a lesson in the indiscriminate nature of joy and its effusive spread.

Their colorful wings, bearing patterns as unique as fingerprints, can be seen as emblems of individuality within the collective mission of proliferation. It is a quiet reminder that while our paths are beautifully singular, our destinies are shared, each one of us contributing to the grand design of wellbeing.

In our own lives, moments when joy is carried from one heart to another, makes us like butterflies instrumental for building a more fecund and jubilant world. Through small gestures and grand overtures, we will nourish the flowering of potentials, deepen bonds, and realize happiness no less for ourselves than others.

As the butterfly's role in the garden is intrinsic and unquestioned, so is our capacity to pollinate our communities with joy. It takes but a single insect to begin a chain reaction of growth, and likewise, a single act of kindness to spark a movement of love and positivity across the human garden.

Consider then how vital our roles are, like butterflies, in this shared ecosystem of elation. We were born with wings – as part of our innate human ability to touch lives, to influence, and to create waves of joy that crash gently away on the shores of other beings. And the role of the butterfly is more than that of just a service which it provides as pollinator but an ambassador to happiness, creature that proves to be an ode to the interplay of life.

Let us be inspired by these ambassadors of delight, embracing our responsibility to carry forth joy, understanding that the lives we touch will bloom in response. Let us recognize how, in the depths of nature's simple acts, lie profound truths about our existence and the shared endeavor to cultivate a garden brimming with joy, love, and the sweet nectar of fulfilled lives.

May butterflies abound in all gardens and may joy abound to all lives.

Exploring the Importance of Positive Relationships and Community Support

In the dance of life, as in the complex ballet of a butterfly's journey, there exists a chord so profound yet so natural—the harmonious symphony of relationships and community. It's in this interconnectedness that the nectar of our human experience is richest, that we find the sweetest support for the weight of our wings.

One seldom traverses a landscape of joy without the echoes of laughter, the shelter of companionship, or the reinforcing touch of a kindred spirit. The tapestry of human connection, intricate and resilient, provides the backdrop against which we manifest our fullest lives. Like butterflies in a sunlit meadow, we flit together, apart, yet always within the warmth of the community's gaze.

When times go hard, we may count on our positive relationships to be the zephyrs that float us ashore. There are nowhere better places to seed the happiness other than into the arms of a caring family, in an unfailing support of friends, or in oneness of a bigger community.

Community support extends beyond the immediate to the collective, where we engage in the shared resolve to uplift, to laugh in unison, and to shoulder each other's burdens. These bonds often form the lattice upon which we claim the light, where mutual encouragement acts as sunlight, and understanding serves as rain.

Witness the butterfly, never solitary, always in the subtle company of the breeze, the bloom, and its kin. It reminds us that solitude can be a choice, but isolation is often an illusion. We thrive in communion with others, in spaces where our souls are free to mingle and our joy to echo.

Perchance, in darker moments, when the garden feels barren and the blossoms of companionship withered, the remembrance of past connections can invigorate us. The memory of a handheld, a burden shared, or simply the presence of another, might renew the internal gardens within our tired hearts.

Just as the butterfly does not question the readiness of the flower to receive it, we too must trust in the openness in others to our need for connection. To seek out the warmth of community is not a weakness, but rather an affirmation of the intrinsic nature of our shared humanity.

In the flutter of engagement with our fellows, there is a sublime teaching; joy is amplified when disseminated. The pleasure of triumph, the solace in sorrow—both increase when spread among the threads of a woven community fabric.

Thus, the task before us becomes one of cultivation—of our gardens, of our relationships, and of the support systems that cradle our aspirations. To water these with intention, to nurture them with care, and to cherish the cycles they endure, akin to the seasonal ebbs and flows of the butterfly's habitat.

Let us not be reticent in our communion with those who offer us solace, nor with those to whom we may extend a supportive branch. From the smallest gestures of kindness to the grandiose projects that bind us in common cause, we craft the chrysalis that will one day unfurl into wings of shared contentment.

The butterfly's journey neither begins alone nor ends in solitude; it is cradled within the vibrant ecosystem it helps to sustain. In recognizing our interdependence, we discern the subtleties of giving and receiving that define the nuanced fabric of societal strength.

To foster the soil of community is to sow seeds that will burst forth in moments of need, offering shade and sanctuary. The isle of self is but an illusion, for we are each a beacon in a more extensive network, casting light upon the waves that others tread.

Ever so gently, we are reminded that in the arms of community, we find a resilience not our own but shared. A collective will that buoys us, a chorus of voices that whispers of courage, and a shared vision that calls us toward horizons bright with the ripest of possibilities.

The garden of joy, thus tended, becomes an endless cultivation of relationships and support—an endeavor as vital as it is rewarding. For as each butterfly in its splendor relies upon the embrace of the meadow, so too do we thrive in the embrace of our collective spirits.

Our journey, as reflective of the butterfly's, encompasses not just the individual flight but the conjoined voyages. And in this confluence of paths, hearts, and hands, we glean the true essence of existence—its fullest expression found in the leverage of love and the buoyancy of belonging.

The Dance of Freedom and Happiness

Within the whisper-thin veil of yesterday's cocoon, complications thrived, yet every struggle has led inexorably here: to the triumphant unfurling of wings that beat in sync with a heart now unburdened. Imagine that the air itself shimmers with promise, the thrumming of countless wings resounding as a testament to the joy of release. You now bask in the incandescence of your own growth, for the dance of freedom and happiness isn't a matter of mere motion; it's an assertion of one's own existence, an embrace of the air and sky with a spirit unclad of its former fears. Sustain this bliss, this resonant echo of the laughter of the soul, through the rise and fall of life's unending symphony. This chapter breathes life into our communal revelry, affirms our shared bonds, and imparts an enduring invitation—to take life by its delicate hand and whirl with it, to let your every step carve a memory on the earth that speaks of a freedom earned, a happiness lived fully, and a dance that weaves threads of radiant light through the fabric of being.

Celebrating the Newfound Freedom and Happiness Within

Emerging from the chrysalis of past challenges, one finds themselves in a clearing, bathed in the soft glow of triumph. A sense of freedom swells within the chest—not just a concept, but a vivacious, fertile reality. Here, in this sanctuary of newfound liberty, one begins to dance a dance that reverberates with the purest joy.

Consider the soft flutter of the butterfly's wings, having fought through the constriction of its cocoon and now elegantly poised in the open air. It dances from blossom to blossoming branch, not merely existing but thriving in its liberated state of being. This creature, so delicate yet resilient, epitomizes the essence of our own potential freedom and happiness—the euphoria of stretching our wings after turmoil and toil.

Freedom's joy is multilayered; it is both a release from what once held us and a welcoming into what could be. The shimmering moments of delight that we collect become the gems we string together in a life lived fully. Celebrating this freedom not really identifying with it, but accepting that the potential which is before is limitless. We rise above the realms of uncertain thoughts and apprehension to accept to embrace the blissful self-discovery.

To celebrate is to let happiness cascade through the soul like a sparkling stream, rich with the melody of our life's experiences. There is music in our steps, a rhythm that cannot be silenced when we honor the journey we have navigated with a joyous heart. Our happiness, once dormant within the confines of our previous bindings, blooms like a vivid flower to the warmth of our attention.

Happiness does not visit us; it is born within us, nurtured by our courage to continue through darkness until we find our dawn. The ebb and flow of existence cannot smother this inner light, for with each triumphant beat of our hearts, we synchronize with the pulse of the universe that whispers, "Live, and be happy."

A mosaic of lessons learnt, resilience earned, and beauty of metamorphosis make a joyous story of a person who has burst free their cocoon. Let us therefore rejoice, encourage our core of being to stay afloat in the unpredictability of life and not just only on today but on every incoming day.

Laughter becomes an incantation, a powerful spell that binds us to the present, where our true power lies. Laughter is a companion through which we experience the full spectrum of our emotions, unabashed and unfiltered. It signifies our determination to remain present in the face of adversity, echoing the decision to choose mirth over melancholy.

The tender truth is happiness is an art honed by the brave—the artisans of their fate who paint their canvas with bold strokes of optimism and vibrant hues of ambition. It is the mastery of recognizing the splendor in simple moments and the orchestration of a life imbued with the intention to flourish.

In our odyssey of self, each of us can ignite the same fiery spirit that enables the butterfly to take its first flight. We uplift ourselves and cast a luminous beacon for those who might still be winding their way through their own struggles, signaling the promise of what lies beyond perseverance.

The dance of freedom and happiness is a dance of communion with the soul and a testament to the will that propels us forward. Such a freedom and happiness are like a music for us which communicatively communes with soul - it dances testimony of will which impels it. For the world is a dance to embrace, not watch from the stands. It is the waltz of serendipity, the tango of destiny, and every step we take dents an invincible imprint of our existence on the fabric of time.

This celebratory dance is not solitary; it calls to the kindred spirits around us, inviting them to partake in the exaltation. Together, we become a chorus of joy, painting our collective happiness across the skies, a testament to the shared human experience that binds us.

Our celebration is a perpetual reminder that every challenge we've faced was not merely an obstacle but an opportunity to sow the seeds of our next great joy. With each challenge overcome, our garden of happiness grows lush, each blossom a symbol of personal fortitude and grace.

So let us dance, gracefully and without hesitation, in this space we've created for ourselves—a sacred arena where our freedom fuels our joy, and our happiness liberates others. We dance for the today that we have forged from yesterday's struggles, and for the tomorrows filled with the promise of life's relentless beauty.

May this celebration be a mirror reflecting back to us the immense internal transformation that has occurred. It is the dance of the soul, reveling in the inner chamber where freedom has taken root and happiness blossoms, unbound and wholly vivacious. It is the dance of freedom and happiness within.

And so, the experience goes on as each of us move to the unique rhythm of each a heart bolden thereby at the expanse of skies above. In this moment, we are truly free-truly happy-a breathing homage-weightless, resplendent, and eternally akin to the indomitable spirit of the butterfly.

Sustaining Happiness Through Life's Ups and Downs

In the dance of freedom and happiness, we glide through the air with wings outspread, akin to butterflies that flit from leaf to leaf. We've delved deep into the cocoon's embrace, unwrapped the silk of challenges, and learned resilience's melody. But what remains is the rhythm that keeps our wings fluttering when the skies darken, and the winds change course. It's the steady beat of happiness within that we must hold onto, amidst life's capricious turns.

But the butterflies, those ethereal sprites, certainly do not escape nature's fickleness. They are in tune with the vagaries of weather, the scarceness of nourishment, and the ravenous pursuit by predators. We, too, face life's tempests—our storms may not howl through the air, but they rage within workplaces, homes, and within our hearts. It's in these moments that finding the inner sanctum, a place of tranquility and steadfast happiness, becomes essential.

Happiness, true and abiding, is never something to be scaled but a horizon to be embraced that's ever-present, often obscured by the clouds of circumstance. It's a quiet knowing joy doesn't come full blown from an absence of sorrow, but the richness embracing the full palette of life's offer. We must drink deeply from the experiences that sweeten and those that embitter, for within each lies the nectar of life's wisdom.

In the way of trying to hold on to this state of contentment we stumble again and again, beguiled by the mirage that happiness is an outside possession. But it must be made inside us, in the crucible of our spirits, a light which no wind or rain can put out as long as we care enough to make sure that it stays alive. It lies in the everyday moments—the laughter shared with a friend, the warmth of sunlight on our skin, or the pride of a job well done.

Imagine for a moment that your happiness is a butterfly garden you tend to, with every thought being a seed planted, every action a watering can's sprinkle. Today's choices are the flowers that bloom tomorrow, attracting life's diverse beauty to your haven. Those who understand this do not leave their gardens to chance; they cultivate it with intention and care, understanding that weeds must be pulled, and pests kept at bay.

Even so, the unpredictable still finds its way through the gates. It does not mean that loss, change, disappointment – all enter uninvited tramping down our well-tended rows. It is important that our present-day joy should not be like a fragile flower that crumples at the merest blight but like a robust wildflower that can struggle up through cracks in the rubble. It is a hop, a constant movement that relinquishes neither to the shadow nor to the sun.

One could argue that sustaining happiness is an art—the art of perspective. It is knowing when to hold close the comforts of the past, and when to reach for the beckoning potential of tomorrow. It's discerning the impermanence of our troubles and the everlasting nature of hope. We must anchor ourselves in a mindset that transcends the transient, looking for lessons in the face of hardships, finding growth amidst pain.

Connection, too, is vital in this dance of happiness. Like butterflies that drift on shared breezes, our lives are interwoven with others whose stories echo ours. In community, there is strength, the assembly of hearts that can uplift us when our wings falter. It's through shared joy and sorrow that our path retains its light, even as night encroaches.

As we traverse this intricate waltz of highs and lows, we can adopt practices that stoke the flames of joy. Mindfulness, the graceful art of truly being there, allows us to relish this moment on the dance. It is smelling the rain and feeling it kiss your cheeks with nary a sliver of yesterday or a cloud of tomorrow's worries dampening its glory.

Gratitude is also a friend of happiness. It's an acknowledgment, minuscule and almost imperceptible, a whisper alive in the heart, for the unseen hand that guides the butterfly's journey. Counting one's blessings is a profound essence of power as we name them one by one, in focusing on the abundance rather than the lack. This shift in focus doesn't negate the challenges but envelops them in a larger tapestry of positivity.

In moments of doubt and despair, it is of the butterfly's resilience that one takes comfort. It had a tiny frame, seeming delicate, yet it made up with strength and determination which belied their fragility. Reminder from persistence carried us out of cocoons, propelled us through transformation, pushing us into the expanse of the sky. We remind ourselves we've weathered storms before; we will do so again.

And let's not forget, sometimes sustaining happiness means simply allowing ourselves to be, without agitation for action or the weight of expectation. There is courage in quietude, in resting on a petal and letting the world spin, trusting in the flow of life to carry us forward.

The butterfly doesn't rush from bloom to bloom in desperation— it dances in the light, patient and unfettered.

Remember, no garden is ever in perpetual bloom. There are seasons of bounty and seasons when the earth grows cold and silent. So too will our happiness ebb and flow. But with each passing cycle, with every frost and thaw, we learn, we grow stronger, and we prepare for the next resurgence of life, the next dance.

In this ever-evolving dance of freedom and happiness, let us be like the butterfly—embracing each turn of the music with grace and confidence. Our happiness isn't waiting at journey's end; it's woven into the fabric of each soaring flight, every gentle pirouette, and the restful pause between. It's in the love we give, the kindness we receive, and the beauty we find in the mirror of our lives.

With the knowledge that each step, each beat, and every fluttering wingbeat adds to the beautiful tapestry of a life well lived, let us hop through the sunny days and into the peaceful nights. With the knowledge that each step, beat, and fluttering wingbeat adds to the beautiful tapestry of a life well lived, let us dance, through the sunny days and into the peaceful nights. This is the dance of freedom and happiness—fluid, ever-changing, but always ours to choreograph with the threads of joy that we gather and weave into our days.

Encouraging Readers to Dance Through Life with a Sense of Fulfillment

When a butterfly emerges from its cocoon, it accomplishes more than only soar into the air. Its movement is a tribute to the unspoken melody of liberty that is life. The free-flowing rhythm of this dance becomes the very essence of being. So it must be with us, as we move through the variegated tapestry of our lives, finding the rhythm that beckons to the beat of our own wings.

The dance of life is more than just moving from one place to another; It is the physical expression of the body, satisfaction and pleasure. Your every step, every obstacle, and every celebration of your success is part of the beautiful dance that is you fully hopping through life

Sometimes, the music of our lives plays to a tune of difficulty, the melody harsh, the tempo unpredictable. But even in these moments, there's grace to be found in the dance. It's during these times when our movements become more deliberate, more essential, our resilience the very rhythm that sustains us.

The butterfly's early struggle as it presses against the confines of its chrysalis is worth great considerations. Without this struggle, without this initial dance against the bindings of its former self, it would never develop the strength to fly. Like the butterfly, our struggles can be a powerful prelude to our freedom.

At the heart of fulfillment lies a choice—the choice to honor all phases of our journey. The stillness as much a part of the dance as the leap. When we are still, we are not stagnant. We are listening, we are preparing, we are poised for the next swirl and twirl that life offers up.

The dance through life is a rich, complex narrative—one that we write and rewrite with every step we take. It's about allowing yourself to move to the unique rhythm of your circumstances and the music of your soul's desires. Acknowledging this as the ultimate dance floor allows us to appreciate the partners we meet along the way, the connections we forge, and the joy of movement itself.

Fulfillment does not mean the absence of pain or discomfort, but rather the deep and abiding sense that each turn in our dance has its place. Our missteps, our faltering moves, they are not moments of broken choreography, but opportunities for improvised grace, just waiting to be realized.

In this pursuit, our goal is not to perform a faultless routine but to feel the music deeply and let its resonance guide us. Perfection is not the destination; expressive, authentic movement is. It's the dips and rises, the spontaneity, the experience of the now that enhances the dance's beauty and nourishment to the soul.

Therefore, invite joy into your life, not as a visitor, but as a permanent inhabitant. Let it influence your movements, and in those times when happiness seems a reluctant partner, dance alone with the fortitude that knows joy will return to the floor.

A person's spirituality is just as important as their senses while they dance through life. There are sights, sounds, and smells that contribute to the drape of our daily life evidence. Our senses allow us to communicate, learn, and form relationships. These are the elements that give color and texture to our dance.

Our dance through life reserves it most profound and charged moves for our encounters with others. In the hand extended, the shared smile, the listening ear, we perform a quiet ballet of humanity that reinforces our connection to each other.

Remember the value of those breaks, those breathers in the rhythm of life that let us think as you go. They ground us, returning us to the very center of our being and the reason we dance. It's essential to realize that the dance goes on, even when we feel we can no longer hear the music. There are times when music fades and our steps falter. It's in these silent interludes that our inner strength, our heart's silent beat, becomes our metronome, carrying us forward until the melody resumes.

And as the dance goes on, it evolves. It encompasses every leap of joy, every pirouette around obstacles, every sway with the breeze of change. This evolution is the very essence of the dance of life—a continual process of learning, growing, and experiencing.

Embrace this dance. Embrace the fluttering heart within you that seeks to beat in harmony with the universe. For fulfillment comes in acknowledging every beat, every breath, and every motion in our existence as part of this grand choreography we call life.

Nectar of Gratitude

Similar to how a butterfly's delicate proboscis reaches the source of a flower's nectar, deep sincerity is at the core of being you. Such is the depth of *gratitude* that we may draw from the cup of existence. As we travel through the myriad of challenges and marvels that fashion our lives, we find that each trial can indeed unfurl into a triumph, each adversity can transform into an advantage if we fuel our flight with the nectar of gratitude. As we've journeyed through various stages—cocoon, metamorphosis, the revealing of resilience's wings—we arrive here savoring sweet victory. This chapter unfolds real-life sagas of endurance, evoking the butterfly's own epic traverse from flowering fields to sun-soaked skies, reminding us that in every instance of surmounting strife, there is always space to distill gratitude. It's not just a feeling, it's how we feel and think. Plus, when we see beauty in hard times, our souls lift up to a place where being thankful is always there instead of only showing appreciation for good things. This makes all that we meet more lovely and better too! This potent perspective becomes the sustenance that propels us through the spectrum of life's vicissitudes, leaving trails of transformative change in its wake.

Real-life Examples of Transformative Journeys

As we go through life's many experiences, the butterfly change is a symbol of deep change. In life's long path, there are some who accept hard times like butterflies. They then become bright and powerful after going through difficult situations.

In the landscape of the human soul, there are tales that mirror this metamorphosis in ways that are truly extraordinary. Consider the story of a woman who, after decades in a career that shackled her spirit, found the courage to cast aside her corporate chains. Her cocoon was a comfortable salary, a predictable routine, but within her stirred a restlessness for authentic expression. When she finally allowed herself to confront the unknown, her transformation began. She became an artist, painting the language of her once silenced heart across canvases that spoke to the souls of many.

There's a man whose life exemplified the power of resilience. Diagnosed with a debilitating illness, he was given a grim timeline. But, he decided to see his problem not as a sign of defeat but as something that makes him value life more. He started a charity to help others like him. He turned his pain into hope for them, showing that sometimes problems are not the end but just the start of something new and life-changing in their own right.

We see such examples in the young poet who found within her whispers of trauma the seeds of lyrical beauty. Her past was marred by suffering and silence until words became her escape, her solace, her metamorphosis. Through verses raw and tender, she offered up her story, her transformation touching the lives of those who found solace in the shared experience of sorrow turned to strength.

The old soldier came back from fighting, not with prizes and party cheering. Instead, he had hidden scars on him and a heart carrying the burden of wars that others can't see or feel. His inside trouble was his cover, from which he fought to get out. However, from the depths of his despair, he discovered the balm of connection in the companionship of service dogs, and he opened a sanctuary. His journey from the shadows into light reminds us that we can find a purpose that heals not only ourselves but also those around us.

Amidst these epics of endurance and revival, we find a thread of commonality—a gratitude pervasive and profound. The young entrepreneur, who once slept in cars and skipped meals, now uses his wealth to lift others from poverty. With each individual he helps, he strengthens the tapestry of his gratitude, acknowledging that his past hardships crafted the empathetic heart that beats within his chest.

Definitely, thanks come from the lives of people who have had big changes. The singer who lost her voice and couldn't sing for months is now singing again. Not only are her vocal chords working well, but also she has a lot of joy from having music back in their life. This reminds us all that happiness comes after sadness as well.

The stories abound—a former prisoner who became a legal advocate, the addict now leading recovery groups, the once homeless person who provides shelters. Each narrative is unique, each journey distinct, but the essence of their stories speaks to a shared human experience of rebirth and gratitude.

Let's not leave out the parents who, even when given a death sentence about their child, picked to use each day with affection and mirth rather than fall into sadness. They enjoy every chance they get. They pick the nectar of gratitude from the most bitter blooms, inspiring countless others to find sweetness amidst the thorns of life.

The elegance of these transformative journeys is not in their destination, but in the quiet moments of realization along the way— the spark of change, the embrace of the inevitable, the dance with the uncertain. These are the times when a fresh life starts to grow. At first, it might be weak but gets stronger with each wing movement until the sky calls and lets go of its gentle grasp on earth.

Yes, every story is a little drop in the huge seas of human life. But together they make waves that can move stuck water and inspire other people to start their own changes about thankfulness. By telling these stories, we create a hidden net of friendship and help. This reminds us that our spirits have strength and loveliness built-in.

These individuals, through their patience, their courage, their pain, and their breakthroughs, show us how the juice (nectar) of gratitude enriches life, how it sweetens our perspective, and how it can attract more beauty into our world. Like the butterfly is pulled to a flower, we are also attracted to gratitude's true nature. This makes even bad times or obstacles worth it because they lead us there.

Let these examples stand, then, not as exceptions, but as testaments to the transformative power within us all. As they have found their wings in the vast blue yonder, we too can unfurl the veils covering our potential and soar into the embracing skies of possibility.

So we take these stories into our hearts and allow them to seed the clouds of our own transformations. Even in the rain and sunshine, during good times and bad, while flying or resting we discover our own wings. We learn to be grateful for what life offers from its never-ending miracles.

Illustrating the Universality of the Butterfly Metaphor

The butterfly, that changes beautifully, holds in its big wings the true ideas about growing and starting fresh. The change from a walking caterpillar to an air creature speaks not only of beauty but also of endless trying. In the narrative of our lives, the butterfly metaphor has a unique ability to marry grace with grit, illustrating that the journey through life's difficulties can lead us to an embodiment of gratitude.

This metamorphosis is universal, entwined in the fabric of every culture and creed. It's found in the folklore of remote tribes and in the bustling streets of modern cities. Everyone, regardless of geography, can relate to the sensation of feeling trapped by things circumstances around them. They also experience growing pains and joy of starting fresh after those times end. It's not the natural journey of butterflies that grabs our attention; it's realizing their travels are like ours.

In illustrating the universality of the butterfly metaphor, we recognize that every struggle is a steppingstone towards a greater version of ourselves. Like the caterpillar hidden in the cocoon, we too often exist in a state of vulnerability before we're ready to surface with resilience and grace. It is a testament to the resiliency of the human spirit that we may embrace these stages of transformation with anticipation rather than fear.

The significance of this metaphor extends beyond individual transformation. Consider the transformative power of societies that endure through periods of upheaval. Here, communities bind, much like the silk threads of a chrysalis, reinforcing the shared aspiration for progress. Within this framework, the butterfly does not stand solitary but represents a symphony of individuals each unfolding their wings of change.

Through the flutter of countless wings, there's an orchestra playing the tunes of shared experiences. We are reminded that every journey of metamorphosis, no matter how distinct, carries with it the echoes of universal challenges and triumphs. The butterfly metaphor celebrates not only personal journeys but also the collective passages of humanity itself, a dance of intricate patterns across the sky of existence.

Moreover, this metaphor brings to light the delicate interplay between struggle and strength. The butterfly signifies that the act of pushing through confines—literal and metaphorical—endows us with the fortitude necessary for flight. As we're inclined to recoil from hardship, the butterfly's tale nudges us towards a posture of fortitude, finding nobility in the endurance that precedes the unveiling of one's potential.

Universal, too, is the process of nourishing one's soul with experiences. Like a butterfly flies from one flower to another for nectar, we move through the gardens of our lives enjoying happiness and sadness together. The large number and intensity of our experiences give us special colors on the wings, like butterfly markings. These are always a sign for different journeys in life that we take.

Amidst this journey, gratitude arises as naturally as a butterfly towards the light. Gratitude for transformation, for the myriad lessons hidden within trials, and for the strength found in renewal. This very nectar of gratitude becomes the wellspring of joy that fuels further flights, further aspirations, and a steady acknowledgement of the blessings threaded throughout even the most tumultuous times.

Touching upon the realm of love and loss, the silhouette of the butterfly is both delicate and poignant. Each wingbeat might be interpreted as a heartbeat, a tender evocation of life's fragility and its inherent magnificence. It signifies the courage to release the past and embrace the present, heralding new beginnings irrespective of the pain of the endings that came before.

Occupying spaces between light and shadow, the butterfly metaphor unfolds into the acknowledgment that even in periods of darkness, we are en route to luminescence. It speaks to the soul that feels entangled in the night, promising that dawn is intrinsic to the cycle of life, and with it comes an iridescent array of possibilities.

Within the universality of the butterfly metaphor, we also discover the celebration of diversity. Just like every type of butterfly has special designs, each human life is a complex cloth with unique events. The metaphor invites us to honor the richness that diversity brings, recognizing the strength and beauty inherent in the variegated patterns of human existence.

There is solace found within the silent flutter of wings—a language understood by all, irrespective of the spoken word. This commonality invites a silent concert of souls, an unspoken communion that transcends barriers constructed by language, culture, or circumstance. It serves as the whispering reminder that the very essence of life is transformation, and it is a journey not undertaken in isolation but in the shared company of millions.

As we delve deeper into the rhythm of the butterfly's journey, our own narratives start to weave parallels that resonate with a profound sense of inherent truth. This universality beckons us to take wing with a heart full of gratitude, harnessing the nectar distilled from each of life's offerings, and to elevate from solitary experiences into the vast expanse of shared understanding and collective growth.

In the end, butterfly comparison isn't just about how lovely it looks but also says beauty is there when something changes. It shows that all parts of life have a kind chance to change. It also softly pushes us closer to light and tells the quiet hope we can find freedom in turning into new things everywhere, anytime again or forever more.

The Butterfly's Journey and the Posture of Gratitude

Life's experiences are like a colorful cloths drape, and the journey of the butterfly shows how thankfulness can grow - it's something delicate yet strong. This attitude is just as important to our spirit as wings are to butterflies themselves. The butterfly teaches us that gratitude is not merely a fleeting thought, but a steadfast stance we adopt, just as it alights upon a flower with intention and poise.

Consider the unassuming caterpillar, whose very existence is an uncharted map of potential. Unburdened by foresight, it feeds, grows, and shapeshifts its way into a cocoon, a sanctuary of transformation. Herein lies the embryonic birthplace of gratitude; the chrysalis harbors and nurtures transformation that isn't visible to the eye but is, nonetheless, poised to unfurl in a spectacle of resilience.

What emerges from the chrysalis extends beyond the tactile - a diaphanous being bedecked in patterns etched over time. The butterfly doesn't dwell on the confines of its previous form. Instead, it stretches its wings, imbued with tacit gratitude for the pliability of its past. It is in this moment of unveiling that gratitude is both the acknowledgment of change and a silent ovation to growth.

The journey of the butterfly is neither straightforward nor serene. It pulses with trials, from inclement weather to the pursuit of sustenance. Yet even as it navigates these vicissitudes, the butterfly surrenders to the current of life, trusting in the invisible thermals that guide its flight. There's an inherent gratitude in this surrender—a recognition that the journey's beauty and its challenges are inextricably linked.

Likewise, we encounter our own storms, our paths rife with unpredictable gusts that threaten to deter us. In these moments, beckoning gratitude into our hearts is much like the butterfly resting on a petal in repose, weathering the wind. We, too, can rest in the assurance that each challenge is a vector towards growth, and we can be grateful for the strength we garner as we flutter through adversity.

Our journey have lots of meeting points with different people. Some are short and some last a long time in our lives. Everyone gives a bit of knowledge, feeling or love that makes us more complete. Here, the butterfly's propensity to pollinate from flower to flower becomes a guiding principle, reminding us to be thankful for the cross-pollination of relationships that shapes our being.

Seeing butterflies moving from one flower to another, you can't help but feel moved by their gentle yet determined actions. These kind gestures start something new and help everything near them grow. It's a peaceful song that shows how all living creatures are linked. It also asks us to be thankful for the help we give and get from each other. Gratitude makes life a place where happiness and beauty grow easily.

Life is brighter when we think not just about where we are now, but also about where our journey began. The trip of a butterfly, like its simple start and perfect finish shows that we should always be thankful for where life takes us. The canvas of the sky is witness to the butterfly's altitudes achieved and the vast distances traversed, each flap of the wing a grateful stroke on the azure.

Amidst our own ascension, we glean lessons in gratitude from the butterfly's silent rhythm—each drop of nectar savored, every breeze appreciated. The butterfly does not pine for yesterday's garden or fret over tomorrow's weather. It exists in a state of presence, collecting moments of gratitude like precious nectar from the present's bloom.

As the butterfly soars, it reveals another aspect of gratitude—the vulnerability in displaying one's true colors. For each pattern, each hue upon a butterfly's wing is a testament to its unique journey, as every scar, laugh line, or crease on our own visages is a marker of our personal pilgrimage. We can grasp gratitude for our individual stories, for the authenticity they bestow upon us.

And what of the quiet? The profound stillness that descends upon the butterfly as it rests, wings folded, upon a dew-dappled leaf at dawn. Here, gratitude finds its reflection in the still waters of introspection, a serene acknowledgment of life's ephemeral beauty. We're summoned to cherish the silence, the quiet reverence for the cycles of life that propel us from dawn to dusk.

In the grand choreography of the butterfly's existence, each flutter, each pause conspires to sustain the majesty of life's ballet. This elegant creature, vested with the wisdom of transformation, prompts us to embrace a posture of gratitude curating each experience as if it were a rare and precious bloom in the gala of existence.

There is a tender grace in acknowledging the layers of our personal epochs—each struggle, each joy, and the nuanced spaces in between. The butterfly's easy change from caterpillar to flying traveler teaches us that thankfulness is like smooth silk weaving throughout life. It joins moments with memories, pain into beauty and fight with success.

And so, as we draw lessons from the butterfly, let's exhale gratitude with each beat of our wings. Every altitude attained, every horizon explored, is but a fragment of the grand odyssey. With the posture of gratitude nestling within our hearts, may we spread our wings and surge forward, with the resolve to make the journey as enriching as the destination itself.

With these thoughts, the nectar of gratitude presents itself not just as a balm but as the very sustenance of our journey—a journey marked by resilience, wrought with beauty, and anchored by the unwavering wings of gratitude. May we embrace it as fully and freely as the butterfly embraces the boundlessness of the sky.

The Flight That Never Ends

As we get near the end of our trip, for good has changed from being in a silk case to appearing often stunning that is made by butterfly wings. But it's in this part called "The Flight That Never Ends" where we find the core of lasting things while searching for our reason, strong spirit and happiness. A butterfly's flight is not just about moving its wings or exploring new places, it's always a journey of learning and change. Just like the never-ending travel of our human heart.

We build, piece by piece, a foundation for lasting happiness not through ephemeral wins but through the accumulation of wisdom, love, and experiences that weave the tapestry of our lives. This chapter is your guide to embracing this boundless flight, urging you to rise above the transient and dive into the transformative infinity that life offers. Like a butterfly, our journey may end. But its beauty and the lessons of life can inspire us to live strong with purpose, toughness and more happiness that lasts forever.

Focusing on the Positive Aspects of Life

Within the gently stirring stillness of dawn, the butterfly emerges, its colors a vivid testament to nature's optimism. Much like this delicate creature, we, too, awaken each day to a landscape ripe with potential. Focusing on the positive aspects of life is an art, a conscious choice that paves the way for something beautiful and liberating. It is here, in this chapter, we explore how to harness this perspective, forever in pursuit of the flight that never ends.

To focus on the positive requires a reshaping of vision—a shift like the precise and remarkable change from caterpillar to butterfly. It needs a look that can find the tiny bit of light in the darkness, or just one flower blooming among many dead plants. The butterflies trip may seem a bit too much, but it shows us that wanting more even when things are hard is very important for getting better.

One might ask, how does one maintain this focus amidst the tumult of daily life? The key lies in the richness of small triumphs. There is enduring beauty in acknowledging the joy of the morning sun after a night of storm, or the laughter shared with a friend during an ordinary afternoon. These moments, easily overlooked, are the threads that weave the intricate tapestry of positivity in life.

Take in the freshness of a new chance, like how a butterfly stretches its wings for their first flight. Every breath can be a source of hope, a spark for good changes. Our lives happen in these breaths, a regular message that good feelings are as easy to find as the air we need. Adopt a stance that eagerly anticipates discovery and joy, and watch as your world expands in response.

Our own personal narratives are enriched by a conscious acknowledgment of the positive steps we take. Like the butterfly instinctively knows the direction of its next flower, trust in the process of acknowledging your growth. Journaling, meditating, or simply reflecting on daily achievements serves as an affirmation of progress, which in turn, attracts more positive outcomes.

Yet focusing on the positive is not merely blind optimism. Instead, it's a balanced understanding that while shadows exist, they serve to accentuate light. Resilience and understanding emerge when we accept the entire spectrum of life's experiences while choosing to see the love, beauty, and potential available to us. Our thoughts are powerful— when we concentrate them on positive aspects, we spark changes in our lives that mirror the magnificent transformation of butterflies.

Cultivating gratitude is like planting a garden in which positivity flourishes. Each day provides a new harvest of blessings, each tiny or tremendous, ripe for thanksgiving. Let gratitude be your daily ritual, an offering to the universe, acknowledging that even in trials, there remains much to appreciate.

When viewed in a good light, even wrong moves turn into useful tips instead of things to feel bad about. Like the butterfly doesn't think about its old cocoon, we can also see our past like a strong shell. It once kept us protected and changed who we are until finally let go to fly free in life. Connection—to oneself, to others, and to the world—is a source of positivity that's as abundant as it is powerful. Foster these connections like a butterfly tends the flowers it pollinates. Let every interaction spread the potential for happiness, learning, and mutual growth, sowing seeds for a greater future.

Remind yourself of life's potential by observing the butterfly's carefree dance. Its flight, seemingly whimsical, is a precise and purposeful journey, ridden by wind gusts and softened by sunlight. Similar carefree moments in our lives, when savored, can provide a sense of freedom and lightness that elevates our perspective.

Instilling positivity in life's difficulties is like flying through different types of weather. The butterfly doesn't fight the wind; it welcomes it and lets itself be taken to its next place. Let life's uncertainties take you to surprising happiness and experiences. Sometimes, it is when you give in to the journey that positivity shows its best side.

Envision a reality where hope is the horizon and positivity the path that leads to it. Craft your days with intent, as a lepidopterist tends to a garden, creating an environment for the most vibrant butterflies to thrive. Enrich your surroundings with affirmations, nurturing relationships, and experiences that reinforce an uplifting outlook.

By changing our view to what's good, we don't just change how things are for ourselves. We also affect the people around us too! Butterfly wings, though small and weak can cause big change. This is similar to how people's good actions which influence others in a strong way. When we rise up, it raises others in a gentle lift of our climbing.

Let the seasons of life unfold as they will, for even in the winter of hardship, a positive spirit remains an undying flame. It's this flame, this perseverance of warmth, that encourages us when the chill of adversity attempts to still our beating wings. The essence of an optimistic heart is the antidote to the frost of despair.

So, keeping our eyes wide open to the beauty in every moment, we need to keep going. Not stopping because life can have good and bad times. Like the butterfly, our trip has no end. There is always a new sky to discover, another limit to touch - the good things in life, an everlasting and exciting chance for us all.

Building a Foundation for Lasting Happiness

As we've gone through the story of the butterfly's life, from being in its cocoon to flying high up into the sky, we learned more than just about how they change shape. We found out what true happiness is all about too. This hard-to find state isn't just a coincidence. It is formed like soft clay by careful hands that can handle the process with patience.

Happiness, much like the vibrant wings of our gentle guide, requires a foundation robust yet flexible enough to sustain the capricious winds of life. It's not merely about the colors we display in moments of triumph but the resilience of our wings in the face of adversity. As such, building this foundation demands that we look inward, to the bedrock of our soul, and outward, to the environment we shape around us.

Reflect upon the quiet strength found within the intricate design of the butterfly's wings; they are a testament to the fact that resilience is integral in the pursuit of lasting happiness. Enduring the elements, they remain lithe, an organic premise that our own happiness shouldn't be rigid but adaptive to the undulating rhythms of our existence.

Consider the butterfly's journey—there is wisdom in the simplicity of its flight, a serene acceptance of the cycle of blossoming and wilting flowers. In our lives, the conception of long-term joy takes root in the gardens of acceptance, where we appreciate the transient nature of each moment, no matter its hue.

Authentic happiness flourishes in the soils of mindful presence, where we absorb the full spectrum of life's offerings. When we let go of the past or worry about the future, and focus on now instead, we get a taste of life that makes us feel truly alive.

Helping this hard-to-find feeling grow needs constant practice of thankfulness. Just like butterflies go to flowers for food, we need always remember and partake in the good-giving ceremony that's all over our way. So, our happiness comes not from looking for more things but by seeing the plenty that is around us.

Strength in community cannot be understated—witness the synchronized ballet of a kaleidoscope of butterflies, each independent yet part of a more significant tapestry. Bonds of trust and compassion constitute the underpinnings of a joyful life. In our interdependence, we discover the fortitude to carry on, even when the skies grow tempestuous.

Maintaining a state of contentment asks that we accept change not as a harbinger of fear, but as the cadence to which life dances. Transitions, though often laden with uncertainty, present an atlas of unseen paths, each a potential avenue to new joy. How we chart this course depends on our willingness to embrace the very essence of change.

The butterfly does not rush its metamorphosis, and neither should we hasten our journey towards a joyful existence. Patience is the watchful guardian at the gates to happiness. It teaches us that unfolding wings of joy requires time and cannot be forced, for the most exquisite things often demand the longest wait.

Even as we unfold our own wings, it's vital to engage in the deliberate practice of self-reflection, to peer into the mirrors of our past without dwelling there. Knowing where we've soared and faltered gives us the wisdom to navigate our present and future. Our happiness emerges, phoenix-like, from the understanding and forgiveness of self.

Amid the colorful chaos of life, maintaining balance is key. It is the equilibrium between giving and receiving, the delicate harmony between obligation and indulgence, which sustains our happiness. Imagine the butterfly's poised flight, a balancing act between gravity and grace, embodying the delicate equilibrium we strive for. Finding happiness in everyday things, like the quiet whisper of a breeze or the warm touch of sunlight, is similar to how butterflies enjoy small drops of dew. When we learn to enjoy the simple things, this makes us happy even if big or new surprises go away.

Lastly, don't forget that finding happiness can't be separated from finding a purpose in life.

As the butterfly serves the world through pollination, our own fulfillment is intertwined with the contributions we make. A life punctuated with purpose affords a buoyancy, lifting us over life's tempests into the clarity of unburdened skies.

The flight that never ends is not an aimless sojourn but a purposeful journey propelled by the very wings we cultivate through acts of resilience, gratitude, and mindful presence. It is a voyage that begins with every sunrise, a reminder that each day presents a renewed opportunity to soar toward the horizons of our happiness.

And as our narrative parallels the butterfly's flight, we realize that building a foundation for lasting happiness is not a destination but a practice. It's the smart thing we do to connect our experiences, thoughts and actions into a beautiful picture of living life right. This shows that happiness lasts forever if we reach for it

Summarize Key Lessons and Takeaways from the Butterfly's Metaphorical Journey

Throughout the winding paths and the upward spirals of a butterfly's journey, much has been revealed about the poignancy of our own human sojourn. Just like a butterfly comes out of its cocoon, we need to accept our troubles. We should see them as things necessary for us to grow stronger.

The cocoon, a symbol of life's difficulties, shows us how to be strong. When the butterfly is fighting to get out, it makes its wings stronger. Just like that, we make our spirit strong by not giving up even when things are tough for us. Understanding that life's problems are not to limit us but make us better is important.

Then there's the epoch of transformation—the metamorphosis that speaks of the discomfort change invariably imports. Our lives, much like the developing butterfly, demand transformation, and it's within this disquiet of change that the most profound growth can take hold.

Deeper still is the beauty wrought by trials. Indeed, adversity carves into us a certain depth, an essence that radiates a personal beauty and strength once unimaginable. It is the storms weathered, the dark nights endured, that sculpt our soul's most captivating features.

Resilience, akin to the emergent butterfly's wings, is not a trait with which we are all naturally endowed. Rather, it is a facet of character that we cultivate through consistent challenge, developing in us a robustness akin to the butterfly's remarkable ability to adapt to shifting environments.

We've explored too the propulsive force that resilience can exert on our lives. Like fledgling wings unfurling, resilience in us can be nurtured, drawn out, and fortified to confront life's setbacks and uplift us towards our personal aspirations.

The act of soaring beyond our limits helps us face the fears and doubts that hold us back. We want to be like the butterfly, flying smoothly - a time where we get free from our thought limitations and spread out into wide skies of discovering ourselves. Storms will arise, certainly, as they do on the butterfly's path. Yet, in these disturbances, there's a valuable lesson in seeking calm within chaos. It's in the eye of the storm that the butterfly—and we—find the most profound tranquility.

Our wings are not just for resilience but for practical acts of transformation as well. The strategies we employ to evolve and enhance our lives, to chart a course for lasting change, mirror the butterfly's intuitive navigational skills.

And what of the gardens we frequent? The joy of being connects with the way a butterfly alights on flowers, enjoying the nectar while inadvertently sowing the seeds for more beauty to bloom. It reflects the importance of fostering positive relationships and cultivating supportive communities.

In our dance of freedom and happiness, there is much to learn from the butterfly's unburdened flight. Celebrating our transformation comes with the acceptance that happiness is a dynamic dance, one that ebbs and flows through every season of life.

Gratitude, much like the nectar the butterfly seeks, nourishes us. It's in this posture of thankfulness that even the ordinary flapping of wings is recognized as the magnificent flight it truly is—a transformative journey marked by grace and gratitude.

In the end, we know that a butterfly's flight and even our own journey never really stops. Every part of life has fresh places to discover, new gardens to care for and more skies in the sky. It's a lovely round trip - always growing, being tough and happy.

As we reflect on these lessons, let us embrace the realization that our own flights of freedom are already underway. With a strong mindset and open to happiness, we can live life not just following duties but really reaching our potential.

Let this summarization of the butterfly's metaphorical journey serve not as an end, but as an invitation. An invitation to recognize the beauty of our own transformation, to spread our wings with courage, and to take flight into the boundless skies of our own unending journey.

Encouraging Readers to Embrace Their Own Flight of Freedom

Now, at the end of our journey together let's look to where the endless sky is calling. Here lies the stretch where you, much like the butterfly, are urged to embrace the freedom that is inherently yours. It's not just the act of flying that we admire in these delicate creatures, but the boldness to launch into the unknown with wings spread wide.

The notion of freedom is as varied in its expressions as the patterns etched upon a butterfly's wing—unique, intricate, and personal. To live free is to make choices that resonate deeply with your truest self. It's to live unencumbered by the cocoons we so diligently spun around ourselves in the guise of comfort and certainty.

Picture yourself at the side of a green field with lots of wildflowers swaying in light wind. This is the time when you can pick to move ahead, leave behind the fears that held you back before. You have gathered strength from your struggles, wisdom from your changes, and beauty from the adversities you've weathered. These are your wings.

Embracing your flight does not mean you won't encounter turbulence. Just like the butterfly that goes through storms, you'll learn inside yourself there is peace and a strong spirit to help carry on. Use this inner power and let it lead you to fly past the limits that used to hold you down.

Friend, freedom is more than just not having rules. It means we can make our own decisions.

It's the decision to rise each morning and pursue the joy of simply being. To spread happiness as freely as the butterfly pollinates the flowers, and to cultivate relationships that support and uplift you.

Your dance through life should be filled with a rhythm that matches the beat of your heart, a choreography that celebrates every moment of freedom and happiness you encounter. This flight is not one of mere survival, but one of thriving, of finding the melody in the everyday occurrences that make life so rich.

Let gratitude be the nectar that fuels your flight. Yes, the sweet drink that powers your journey. Use it like you would from a big well, and let it help you on your trip. Your path is a transformative passage that holds the potential to inspire not just yourself, but those who watch you glide through the air with effortless grace.

The flight of freedom is an ongoing voyage—an infinite loop that echoes the timeless cycle of life and renewal. You are not simply moving away from what was, but also soaring towards what can be. With each beat of your wings, you are scribing your path across the sky, painting it with the vibrant hues of your experiences.

You hold the power to make a plan for personal growth that matches your dreams. You can use what you've learned to be part of your daily life. This change that you can do is a secret key to open doors maybe you didn't even know existed.

Now, let's not be afraid of the truth that there will be days when the wind stops blowing. On those days our wings may feel heavy. These are not the days to hide away, but these should be times when we sit and gather energy. We must think about how far we've come along our journey and dream bigger for what comes next.

Your flight of freedom is uniquely yours, but remember, it is also a part of a grander choreography—a dance shared with the many who journey alongside you, though their flights may take different shapes and courses. Celebrate not just your flight, but the collective dance of liberation and joy we all partake in.

The butterfly's journey is a constant ebb and flow, a series of new beginnings that stem from every ending, and so is yours. As we come to a close on this written journey, remember that the metaphorical flight we've explored is cyclical, a narrative without a true ending, only ever-changing chapters.

Take this moment. Let it be a defining one where you commit to not just the idea of flight, but to the practice of it. Let your life show the beauty that comes when you decide to leave the ordinary and take a chance on extraordinary level of freedom.

May you always find courage in the quiet of the cocoon, strength in the silken threads of change, and joy in the vastness of clear blue skies. Here's to your flight—a journey that indeed never ends, but rather, transforms with each beat of your ever-resilient wings.

In the end, living a meaningful life with strength and joy isn't only something we want. It's an ongoing story created by the decisions we make, opportunities we try out and freedoms which encourage us to act. Make your journey last, make it lovely and a part of you.

Closing Thoughts on Living a Life Filled with Purpose, Resilience, and Happiness

On the final analysis, we should approach the end of this journey, with considering the need to look back to understanding what living with a purpose means. To stand strong in tough times and create a happy place inside ourselves can make our lives better and more fulfilled when all things are considered. Like a butterfly, we have come out from hiding and now soar high. Like it always spreads its wings to explore new places, we also keep growing every day to find what our own potential really is.

Each fluttering wingbeat is a testament to the butterfly's incredible metamorphosis – an echo of the transformations we have explored together. The paths to purpose, resilience, and happiness are seldom straight; they curve and jolt with the complex geometry of life's own design, and therein lies their beauty.

Living with purpose is not all about setting a final goal, but more like guiding our actions based on what we care most for and enjoy. It means we can look for meaning in our everyday actions, and just like a butterfly chooses flowers to collect nectar from one flower at time. No matter how small or short-lived the experience is, it still has value.

Resilience is not just about having the power to keep going, but also being kind enough to let go of things that are no longer helpful in our life. Like a butterfly that has to leave its cocoon, we also need to get rid of old ways in order for new things happen. It's clinging not to how the wind should blow but setting your wings to ride it wherever it may go.

So, happiness doesn't become a place we must get to. It becomes someone who stays with us on our journey. It shows up in the calm times when we bond with ourselves and others. It also happens during a laugh shared by a friend, or when someone hugs us gently who they care for—or even while being alone to think about things deeply.

Indeed, we've learned from our winged guides that happiness is not a steady state but a dynamic play of light and shadow. It is about finding equilibrium amidst the ever-shifting clouds, about accepting the rain as much as we cherish the sunlight piercing through them.

Embrace change as the butterfly entrusts its transformation to the unfolding process of nature. Accept that pain, though unwelcome, has the power to sculpt and refine us. One cannot imagine the butterfly ruing its days within the cocoon; rather, it emerges with wings wide, eager to ascend.

The flight that never ends is symbolic of the ongoing nature of our own growth and evolution. Each fork in the road, each decision, every challenge, and joy is yet another beat of our wings, pushing us forward into tomorrows filled with undreamt possibilities.

Even as our path converges with storms and the inevitable headwinds of life, remember that the butterfly, delicate as it may seem, navigates turmoil with an inherent wisdom. It adjusts, adapts, and finds a way to let the tempest lift it higher.

In spreading our wings, let us take this wisdom to heart. Let us approach each day with the understanding that we have the tools to float on the breeze, to dance in the wake of upheavals, and to land softly with sureness and agility.

Let us also not forget that the simple act of flapping our wings can have profound effects. Just like a butterfly whose quick wings can change the weather even far away, tiny changes we make to ourselves can have effects that go beyond us. They may help create better conditions in many places and odd ways which might not be completely clear to us always.

To live with thanks is to understand that all moments, good or bad ones too, are a present opened in the course of time. This means to keep all the different experiences in life, learn from each one and continue going forward. It's like having a happy heart that isn't stopped by anything.

As we fold this final page, consider the flight of the butterfly not as a journey with an end, but as a promise of continuity, an eternal cycle of beginnings and discoveries. It's a reminder that purpose, resilience, and happiness are not destinations, but the manner in which we travel – unfettered, ever ascending, and profoundly alive.

The smartness of the butterfly isn't in the far it goes but how pretty its flying is. In every heartbeat and dream we have; we are connected to the beauty of life. By sharing our hopes and dreams with others, it shows us how strong life can be.

So, with our hearts full of joy and souls free to move as we like taking deep breaths in life; we continue. Each one of us travels on a journey carrying some unique experiences which adds colorful threads into the ever-expanding human blanket made up by all together.

With eyes lifted to the horizon and souls anchored in the here and now, our journey – this flight that never ends – is a beautiful affirmation of life's most enduring dance.

Additional Resources

In the spirit of growth and continuous learning, this chapter offers an expansive reservoir of literature and wisdom that can complement the transformative journey you've been exploring. Imagine a colorful garden of texts, each petal and leaf bursting with insights akin to the enrichment a butterfly seeks from one flower to the next. These recommended books on personal growth are curated lanterns in the pursuit of enlightenment, standing as sentinels that have witnessed countless metamorphoses and now whisper secrets to those willing to immerse themselves in their pages. Interlaced among these tomes are inspirational quotes, the distilled essence of human experience captured in a few potent words. They serve as sparks, ready to ignite the resilience and beauty inherent in each of us. Envision guided exercises that offer a scaffold for reflection, inviting you to alight upon insights and integrate them into the very fabric of your being—tools for implementation, ensuring the seeds of wisdom you've gathered germinate into action. Together, these resources are counterparts to the resting places butterflies find among the branches, spots of reprieve and nourishment on their ever-forward flight.

Recommended Books on Personal Growth:

As we've looked at the complicated butterfly life cycle, you may see connections between its different stages and your own personal journey. To further nurture the seeds of personal growth planted through our exploration, I've compiled a list of essential readings that will guide you along the serpentine path toward the sunlight of your potential.

- First on the list is a book that echoes the resilience of the cocoon stage, teaching the beauty of tenacity in the midst of life's constrictions. "Grit: The Power of Passion and Perseverance" by Angela Duckworth champions the idea that the unyielding quest to follow through with our ambitions is a paramount force behind success.

- Another treasure is "The Road Less Traveled" by M. Scott Peck, which begins with the profound truth that "Life is difficult." This tome takes you by the hand down a path of self-discovery, examining the idea that once we accept and embrace life's hardships, we can begin the work of growth.

- For those experiencing the tumultuous winds of change, "Who Moved My Cheese?" by Spencer Johnson is a delightful parable that highlights the inevitability of change and the importance of adaptability. Through its simplicity, it offers comforting guidance on how to anticipate and enjoy the shifting landscapes of life.

- While discussing the beauty born of adversity, it's crucial to consider "Man's Search for Meaning" by Viktor E. Frankl. In this moving account, Frankl, a psychiatrist, and Holocaust survivor, illustrates how finding purpose in the most heartbreaking circumstances can lead to personal enlightenment.

- In the spirit of the butterfly's resilience, "Rising Strong" by Brené

- Brown is a vital addition to your library. Brown invites us to be courageous, to embrace vulnerability, and to rise from our falls with newfound wisdom.

- To further support the cultivation of resilience touched on in earlier chapters, "The Resilience Factor" by Karen Reivich and Andrew Shatté provides practical advice and exercises for bouncing back from life's inevitable setbacks.

- As we ponder breaking free from limitations, "The Four Agreements" by Don Miguel Ruiz presents a powerful code of conduct that can lead to personal freedom and true happiness. Its wisdom helps dismantle the shackles we place upon ourselves.

- For navigating through life's storms, "Wherever You Go, There You Are" by Jon Kabat-Zinn is an invaluable source. It introduces mindfulness as a tranquil harbor against the squalls, teaching that peace can be achieved in any moment, simply by being fully present.

- Taking practical steps for transformation requires a starting point, and "Atomic Habits" by James Clear is that foundation. Clear describes how the accumulation of small changes leads to remarkable results, a perfect parallel to a butterfly's journey from larva to majestic, winged creature.

- Emphasizing the joy of living, "The Book of Joy" by Dalai Lama and Desmond Tutu delves into the heart of what it means to truly feel joy, even in the face of life's relentless trials. Their poignant conversations and infectious laughter are a testament to the indomitable human spirit.

- One cannot speak about transformation and the dance of freedom without acknowledging "The Power of Now" by Eckhart Tolle. Tolle invites us into the dance of life urging us to lead with a consciousness rooted firmly in the present moment.

- And as we bask in the nectar of gratitude and reflect on our life's transformations, "Thanks! How Practicing Gratitude Can Make You Happier" by Robert A. Emmons, delves deeply into the science and psychology behind gratitude, enriching our understanding and application of this powerful state of being.

- "The Alchemist" by Paulo Coelho offers a timeless narrative about following one's dreams and listening to the heart's direction. It's a story imbued with the essence of the journey we've discussed, a poignant reminder that the treasure we seek often lies within.

In conclusion, these readings are like streams feeding into a mighty river of understanding, each book offering unique perspectives and tools to guide you through the seasons of your journey. As you turn their pages, may you discover the unstoppable force of personal growth that resides within you, just as the butterfly emerges with wings unfurled, ready to soar towards the horizon of its aspirations.

Inspirational Quotes

Within the realm of transformation, where the heart dances an intricate ballet with the soul, there echoes a symphony of voices— voices that have traversed through time to nestle into our consciousness and inspire. Through this gathered collection of words, let their whispers fan the embers of your spirit and illuminate your path.

Consider the metamorphosis, the quiet strength it whispers: "Just when the caterpillar thought the world was over, it became a butterfly." These words aren't merely strung together; they represent the silent roar of rebirth, echoing the profound truth that often, our end is just our beginning. Hold this close when each sunset of your life seems final.

In the embraces of adversity, find solace in the profound: "What the caterpillar calls the end of the world, the master calls a butterfly," a testament to perspective's power. It transforms a waning phase into the promise of wings. Let this redefine your storms as skies waiting for your flight.

Battle through your cocoon with vigor, lean on timeless encouragement: "Strength does not come from winning. Your struggles develop your strengths. When you go through hardships and decide not to surrender, that is strength." These words are a testament to the journey that shapes you more than the destination ever will.

Allow the prospect of change to fill your sails with this thought: "Change is the essence of life; be willing to surrender what you are for what you could become." Remember, like the butterfly, you are destined not to crawl but to soar amidst the blooms of opportunity.

As you navigate through storms, find your calm within the chaos:

"In the midst of movement and chaos, keep stillness inside of you." This demonstrates the art of inner peace, the silent eye found within life's tempests. Let this piece of wisdom guide you to tranquility amongst the turbulence.

Recall that your wings of resilience were built to outlast: "He who has a why to live can bear almost any how." The journey ahead may be steeped in mist, but with a steadfast reason, you can climb higher than the fog to where the sun smiles upon your path.

When self-doubt shadows your potential, shine forth with belief: "Believe you can and you're halfway there." Hold this conviction as your beacon, the flickering flame that ignites the fuel of your endeavors and propels you from dreams to the tangible touch of reality.

Seek joy in the gardens you cultivate along the way, uplifting through the immortal words: "Happiness is not something ready-made. It comes from your own actions." Realize that, like the butterfly's dance from flower to flower, your motion creates a ripple of delight that sways the world around you.

And amid your dance of freedom and happiness, let this morsel of truth be your rhythm: "Freedom is nothing but a chance to be better." The liberation you seek is also an invitation—an invitation to expand, to enhance, to elevate all you touch and all you are.

Embrace the nectar of gratitude with a heart full: "Gratitude turns what we have into enough." This sage phrase shifts our gaze from the pursuit to the present, urging us to savor each drop of now, to cherish the garden of our existence, however wild or cultivated it may be.

As the end of one journey only marks a new embarkation, ponder: "Just like the butterfly, I too will awaken in my own time." No timeline binds the process of becoming; each flutter towards the sun is orchestrated by a tempo unique to you.

In your flight that never ends, this insight carries weight: "The only way to make sense out of change is to plunge into it, move with it, and join the dance." The dynamic flow of life need not be an adversary but a partner in an elaborate waltz, one that you both guide and follow with grace.

Lastly, as you take flight, let these words resonate as your constant undercurrent: "Happiness is not the absence of problems, it's the ability to deal with them." Your journey, like that of the awe-inspiring butterfly, may be stitched with storms, but with each beat of your resilient wings, you are painting the sky with your courage.

Carry these quotes, these fragments of long-lived wisdom, in the locket of your heart as you traverse the mosaic of experience and let them be the wind that unfurls your wings with each sunrise. For in the art of heartbeats and horizon chases, you are the maven of metamorphosis—forever unfolding, always becoming.

Guided Exercises for Reflection and Implementation

As we gently close the pages of this book, we get to a place where thoughts turn into real actions. Where big ideas become easy things that can be done. You've ventured through the chapters; now it's time to graft the wisdom of the butterfly onto the living skin of your daily existence. The transformation is not merely to be known but to be embodied, integrated into the fibers of who you are becoming.

Consider first the cocoon clinging to the bare branch. It's an emblem of struggle, a testament to the writhing, vital necessity of pressure. Now, pen in hand, write down the walls of your current cocoon. What binds you? What is the nature of your confinement? Label these walls not as restrictions, but as the contours of your next form. As you write, allow the ink to catalyze a shift in perception, from barrier to chrysalis. Herein lies the seed of metamorphosis.

As you seek to embrace change, draft a record of the discomforts that grip your spirit. They are the pangs of transformation. Detail each one and beside it, scribe an action; a small yet pivotal adjustment that you can initiate today. This list becomes your metamorphosis manifesto, your commitment to navigate the uneasy yet fertile waters of change.

In adversity's shadow, beauty persists—not in spite of struggle, but because of it. With quiet reflection, summon the adversities that have shaped you. Align them side by side with the hidden pearls of beauty they've yielded, crafting a mosaic of strength etched from turmoil. This retrospective can become your personal gallery of fortitude, teaching you that from the ashes of hardship, a more intricate beauty arises.

Resilience is your pair of nascent wings. On a sheet, map the anatomy of your resilience. What are its components? How has it supported you in the gentle and the gale? Chart its growth and cultivate its care, understanding that resilience is not an entity that arrives fully formed but one that is nurtured, branching out organically like the veins of a leaf.

There's boundless power in envisioning the reach of your wings. Imagine the heights they can elevate you to, transcending self-imposed limitations. Write a letter to yourself, from the perspective of your transcendent self, the one who has already soared beyond those heights. Let the words flow with encouragement and be a beacon calling you toward that vantage point above the clouds.

In the face of life's storms, a calm core is the sanctuary we seek. Butterflies find respite even amidst the winds. Construct your own sanctuary in words—a declaration of calm—that you can recite when chaos unfurls its banners. Let it be a litany of peace, an anchor against the tempest's pull.

The act of unfurling your wings requires not just a resolve of spirit but a practical scaffolding. From the abstract beauty of our journey, distill concrete steps for action. Jot down daily practices that inch you closer to the summit of your transformation. This can be as simple as a morning affirmation or a pledge to face one fear each day. Commit to these steps and watch the astonishing unfoldment of your being.

In the quest for joy, your garden awaits its tender. Catalog the elements of joy in your life, the big and the small. Give each its plot in your garden plan and consider how you might water and sustain it. Surround your plot with the companionship of others who, too, seek to cultivate jubilance. This garden grid becomes a working document for the joy you choose to bring into the world, reflecting the interconnected pollination that the butterfly so gracefully enacts.

Freedom and happiness, once tasted, become an insatiable dance. Create your dance card, outlining the steps you'll take each day to sustain and cherish this rhythm. In this composition, permit yourself to swing between the zeniths and the nadirs, recognizing that the music might shift, but the dance endures.

Gratitude is akin to the sweet nectar that fuels the journey. Each evening, as twilight drapes its cloak, take time to note the droplets of gratitude within your day. These scribbles assemble into a personal anthology of thankfulness, a reservoir to draw from when the wellspring feels parched. A mapping of the tender, often overlooked moments that scaffold your soul.

As you prepare to close the chapter on this written voyage, look back on the key insights that resonate most. Capture the essence of these lessons in a personal creed, a testament to the journey you've undertaken and a charter for your continuing flight. Let it be a proclamation of the life you are crafting, one painted with purpose and emboldened by the resilience of the butterfly.

And as you brace for your own incessant flight, draft a vision of the life that unfurls its promise before you. Who will you become as you spread your wings? How does the world alter from your new perspective? Write it as a vivid scene, rich with the hues of hope and the textures of dreams realized. This vision is a beacon to your present self, a portrait of the horizon toward which you are ever soaring.

The art of transformation is to continue becoming, as the butterfly teaches us with its cyclical rebirth. As we part ways with the written word and as your story continues to soar in the boundless sky, let reflection lead to action. The exercises detailed herein are but a beginning, the first brushstroke on the vast canvas of your existence.

Hold fast to the wisdom gleaned, to the kinship with the butterfly's path. For in this companionship, you'll find the strength to embrace the very nature of your journey, discovering that in every end is also the delicate whisper of beginnings. As you fold these pages, embark on your path with the gentle yet unyielding resolve to transform, and in so doing, unlock the very essence of life's unfolding beauty.

References

Brown, B. (2017). Rising strong: how the ability to reset transforms the way we live, love, parent, and lead. Random House.

Bstan-Vdzin-Rgya-Mtsho, Dalai Lama Xiv, Tutu, D., & Abrams, D. (2016). The book of joy. Hutchinson.

Clear, J. (2018). Atomic Habits. Editura Trei SRL.

Don Miguel Ruiz. (2008). The Four Agreements. Hay House Inc.

Duckworth, A. (2016). Grit: The power of passion and perseverance. Scribner.

Emmons, R. A. (2008). Thanks! : how practicing gratitude can make you happier. Houghton Mifflin.

Frankl, V. E. (2020). Man's search for meaning. Rider Books.

Johnson, S. (2018). Who moved my cheese?: An a-mazing way to deal with change in your work and in your life. G.P. Putnam's Sons.

Kabat-Zinn, J. (2023). Wherever You Go, There You Are. Hachette Go.

Paulo Coelho. (2006). The alchemist. Harpercollins.

Reivich, K., & Shatte, A. (2003). The Resilience Factor. Harmony.

Scott, M. (2012). The Road Less Travelled. Rider, , ©8.

Tolle, E. (2000). The power of Now: A Guide to Spiritual Enlightenment. Hodder Headline Australia.

www.ingramcontent.com/pod-product-compliance
Lightning Source LLC
Chambersburg PA
CBHW022057020426
42335CB00012B/728